BTEC Level 3 National Study Skills Guide in Travel and Tourism

Welcome to your Study Skills Guide! You can make it your own – start by adding your personal and course details below...

Learner's name: _____

BTEC course title: _____

Date started: _____

Mandatory units:

_____

_____

_____

Optional units:

_____

_____

_____

_____

Centre name: _____

Centre address:

_____

_____

_____

Tutor's name: _____

Published by Pearson Education Limited, a company incorporated in England and Wales, having its registered office at Edinburgh Gate, Harlow, Essex, CM20 2JE. Registered company number: 872828

Edexcel is a registered trademark of Edexcel Limited

Text © Pearson Education Limited 2010

First published 2010

18 17 16

13 12 11

British Library Cataloguing in Publication Data

A catalogue record for this book is available from the British Library

ISBN 978 1 84690 554 4

Typeset and edited by DSM Partnership
Cover design by Visual Philosophy, created by eMC Design
Cover photo/illustration © Masterfile Corporation
Printed and bound by L.E.G.O. S.p.A. Lavis (TN) - Italy

Acknowledgements

The publisher would like to thank the following for their kind permission to reproduce their photographs:
(Key: b-bottom; c-centre; l-left; r-right; t-top)

Alamy Images: Angela Hampton Picture Library 19, Claudia Wiens 64; Corbis: 74; Getty Images: Fuse 10, Tim Hall 15; iStockphoto: Chris Schmidt 33; Pearson Education Ltd: Steve Shott 28, Ian Wedgewood 57

All other images © Pearson Education

Every effort has been made to trace the copyright holders and we apologise in advance for any unintentional omissions. We would be pleased to insert the appropriate acknowledgement in any subsequent edition of this publication.

Websites

Go to www.pearsonhotlinks.co.uk to gain access to the relevant website links and information on how they can aid your studies. When you access the site, search for either the title BTEC Level 3 National Study Skills Guide in Travel and Tourism or the ISBN 978 1 84690 554 4.

Disclaimer

This material has been published on behalf of Edexcel and offers high-quality support for the delivery of Edexcel qualifications.

This does not mean that the material is essential to achieve any Edexcel qualification, nor does it mean that it is the only suitable material available to support any Edexcel qualification. Edexcel material will not be used verbatim in setting any Edexcel examination or assessment. Any resource lists produced by Edexcel shall include this and other appropriate resources.

Copies of official specifications for all Edexcel qualifications may be found on the Edexcel website: www.edexcel.com

Contents

Popular progression pathways

General qualification	Vocationally related qualification	Applied qualification
Undergraduate Degree	BTEC Higher National	Foundation Degree
GCE AS and A level	BTEC National	Advanced Diploma

Ten steps to success in your BTEC Level 3 National

BTEC Level 3 National

This Study Skills Guide has been written to help you achieve the best result possible on your BTEC Level 3 National course. At the start of a new course you may feel both quite excited but also a little apprehensive. Taking a BTEC Level 3 National qualification has many benefits and is a major stepping stone towards your future career. Using this Study Skills Guide will help you get the most out of your course from the start.

TOP TIP

Use this Study Skills Guide at your own pace. Dip in to find what you need. Look back at it whenever you have a problem or query.

During **induction** sessions at the start of your course, your tutor will explain important information, but it can be difficult to remember everything and that's when you'll find this Study Skills Guide invaluable. Look at it whenever you want to check anything related to your course. It provides all the essential facts you need and has a Useful terms section to explain specialist terms, words and phrases, including some that you will see highlighted in this book in bold type.

This Study Skills Guide covers the skills you'll need to do well in your course – such as managing your time, researching and analysing information and preparing a presentation.

- Use the **Top tips** to make your life easier as you go.
- Use the **Key points** to help you to stay focused on the essentials.
- Use the **Action points** to check what you need to know or do now.
- Use the **Case studies** to relate information to your chosen sector and vocational area.

- Use the **Activities** to test your knowledge and skills.
- Use the **Useful terms** section to check the meaning of specialist terms.

This Study Skills Guide has been designed to work alongside the Edexcel Student Book for BTEC Level 3 National Travel and Tourism (Edexcel, 2010). This Student Book includes the main knowledge you'll need, with tips from BTEC experts, Edexcel assignment tips, assessment activities and up-to-date case studies from industry experts, plus handy references to your Study Skills Guide.

This Study Skills Guide is divided into ten steps, each relating to a key aspect of your studies, from understanding assessment to time management to maximising opportunities. Concentrate on getting things right one step at a time. Thousands of learners have achieved BTEC Level 3 National qualifications and are now studying for a degree, or building a successful career at work. Using this Study Skills Guide, and believing in your own abilities, will help you achieve your future goals, too.

Introduction to the travel and tourism sector

'Dynamic', 'challenging' and 'exciting' are words often used to describe the travel and tourism sector. It's not all fun and games of course, but working in travel and tourism does have excellent opportunities and great appeal.

First and foremost, travel and tourism is a multi-billion-pound business, providing millions of jobs worldwide. It is one of the fastest-growing sectors in the world.

As part of your BTEC Level 3 National course you will investigate the component industries that make up travel and tourism. You will see what they do and how they link together to provide travel and tourism products and services.

For most people, the first thing that springs to mind is holidays. Travel and tourism is not just about holidays, although you will learn about different destinations and about organisations such as tour operators, travel agents and transport providers who are involved in providing your holiday experiences. You will learn how organisations work and the challenges that face them.

Travel and tourism organisations are constantly pushing boundaries to introduce new opportunities for travel. Popular and emerging destinations will be examined around the world. However, the course will also allow you to investigate responsible tourism and the impacts of tourism, including environmental and ethical issues.

Most organisations in travel and tourism are customer-focused, with many front-line jobs available to transform travel and holiday dreams into reality. Skills will be developed to help prepare you for a future role in the travel and tourism sector, perhaps working as a holiday representative, flight attendant or travel consultant.

To give you some idea of the many opportunities available, take a little time to think about the different travel and tourism experiences you have had in the past. These might include:

- a holiday in the UK or overseas
- a day trip to a UK resort or visitor attraction
- a school or college trip or residential.

You may not have realised how many different types of people contribute towards your travel and tourism experience. Using the example of an overseas holiday and breaking it up into different stages, such as booking your holiday, travel arrangements and resort experience, you may come into contact with personnel such as those shown in the following list.

Stages of your holiday	Personnel
Booking the holiday	Travel consultant
	Foreign exchange
At the airport	Check-in staff
	Security staff
	Immigration
	Retail staff
	Despatch staff
On the flight	Cabin crew
In the resort	Holiday representatives
	Tour guides
	Hotel receptionists
	Hotel staff eg bar, restaurant
	Entertainers

These are just a selection of potential job roles you might consider in travel and tourism. In addition, there are many people behind the scenes who develop, plan, sell and operate your holiday. You will learn about these roles, and many more, as part of your course.

Skills for the travel and tourism sector

The travel and tourism sector has an extensive range of job opportunities and can provide openings for people demonstrating many different types of skills. Skills development is built into the programme of delivery and assessment on your BTEC Level 3 National in Travel and Tourism, and the skills you develop will help you in your future career:

Customer service

There are many customer contact roles in travel and tourism, and there is a great deal of emphasis on employees being able to deliver consistently high standards of customer service. This can include face-to-face, written and telephone contact with customers, and can take many forms such as providing information, resolving complaints, offering assistance and dealing with awkward situations.

You may have already developed some customer service skills while carrying out a part-time job, and you will have certainly experienced customer service when out shopping or travelling. It's likely that not all of your experiences will be positive ones. Excellent customer service helps to make an organisation stand out, and can be the deciding factor when a prospective customer is selecting travel and tourism products and services.

All of the travel and tourism employees listed in the left-hand column below will use customer service skills in their day-to-day work. Match up the most likely customer service situation they will deal with in the right-hand column:

uses customer service skills when:		
A flight attendant		dealing with a holidaymaker who has a complaint
A hotel receptionist		making travel and seat reservations
A theme park ride attendant		recommending a suitable holiday to meet customer need
A holiday representative		dealing with passengers who have missed their flight
An airport information assistant		checking in an overseas guest
A travel agent		reassuring a nervous flyer
A tourist information assistant		assisting a disabled visitor
A railway booking clerk		providing information about a destination
An airport passenger services agent		dealing with enquiries about airport facilities

Do your matches look something like this?

- A flight attendant reassuring a nervous flyer.
- A hotel receptionist checking in an overseas guest.
- A theme park ride attendant assisting a disabled visitor.
- A holiday representative dealing with a holidaymaker who has a complaint.
- An airport information assistant dealing with enquiries about airport facilities.
- A travel agent recommending a suitable holiday to meet customer needs.
- A tourist information assistant providing information about a destination.
- A railway booking clerk making travel and seat reservations.
- An airport passenger services agent dealing with passengers who have missed their flight.

As you can see from the examples, customer service skills can take different forms. These include:

- **Face-to-face communication skills**
  Good communication skills mean being able to provide the right information to customers at the right time and in the right way to meet their needs, such as providing information to visitors, calming people down when something goes wrong, and giving instructions.

- **Written communication skills**
  Written communications can include providing written itineraries, producing information for notice boards in a resort, or sending a written

response to a letter of complaint. Whatever the purpose, customers will expect all written communications to be accurate and to meet their needs.

- **Telephone skills**
  An excellent telephone manner is essential to convey a positive impression of an organisation. Travel and tourism employees are taught how to 'have a smile in their voice' and how to convey information or make sales quickly and efficiently.

- **Presentation skills**
  The ability to deliver an effective and memorable presentation could be valuable in your future career. You may find yourself pitching for an event, presenting a business or marketing plan, or delivering a presentation at a sales conference.

- **Complaint handling skills**
  There are many things that can go wrong in the travel and tourism sector. For example, bad weather can disrupt travel plans, accommodation might not meet expectations and advertised facilities might be withdrawn. All of these can result in complaints, and being able to handle these efficiently can make the difference between having a dissatisfied and a satisfied customer.

- **Selling skills**
  Many travel and tourism organisations rely on their staff having excellent selling skills to convert enquiries into sales. Good selling skills will involve finding the right product or service to meet the customer's specific needs.

In addition to customer service skills, there are a number of other skills that are sought after in the travel and tourism sector. These include:

IT skills

Technology is used extensively by most travel and tourism organisations to make bookings, store and retrieve information, create publicity materials and websites, produce reports and communicate effectively.

Being computer-literate has become an everyday expectation, and using technology will be a necessary skill in many jobs.

Language skills

If you can speak other languages, you could put your skills to good use when working overseas or with overseas visitors in the UK.

Administrative skills

Excellent administrators are required by many travel and tourism organisations to maintain records and run the business efficiently. Accuracy, confidentiality and excellent organisational ability are highly sought after by employers.

Teamwork

You may not always notice how teams work together in travel and tourism organisations, but effective teamwork is essential for the smooth running of many travel and tourism services.

There is a saying that 'one bad apple spoils the bunch' and that is certainly true of the travel and tourism sector, where excellent standards of service are important. If one employee performs badly it could affect the whole team's performance.

You will work as part of a team for some of your assignments and will have the opportunity to participate in team activities such as producing a display or planning and delivering a holiday entertainment activity.

Teamwork is one area of the personal, learning and thinking skills that you will develop while you are completing your BTEC programme. See the table on p. 85 for more information on these.

TOP TIPS

Start thinking like a 'mystery shopper' whenever you buy or use travel and tourism products and services. What can you learn from good (and not-so-good) practices?

Step One: Understand your course and how it works

Case study: Using the course to help you decide on a career

Ashwin is attending an interview for the post of tour coordinator with a specialist sports tour operator. He is very keen to get the job as the company specialises in organising trips to sporting events around the world. If he is successful, maybe he'll get the chance to travel to the World Cup or even get to watch a Formula 1 Grand Prix. That would be his dream job.

The first part of the interview is a group activity. As an ice-breaker, candidates are asked to explain why they want to work in the travel and tourism sector. Ashwin has just completed a BTEC Level 3 National in Travel and Tourism. When he began the course he'd had no idea about what he might want to do. He now reflects on the different units he has studied and how they have helped him to realise that this would be a perfect career opportunity for him.

When his turn comes, Ashwin explains about his course, highlighting how different units have given him the chance to find out about all the component industries in the travel and tourism sector and to develop skills that he is now keen to put to good use. He highlights units that are particularly relevant to the role, including Customer Service and Tour Operations, and he concludes that the course has made him want to be part of this dynamic sector. It is a confident response and it emphasises the variety of units Ashwin has studied to give him such a good appreciation of the travel and tourism sector. He feels sure that the interviewers will be impressed.

Reflection point

Why have you chosen this course?

All BTEC Level 3 National qualifications are **vocational** or **work-related**. This means that you gain specific knowledge and understanding relevant to your chosen area. It gives you several advantages when you start work. For example, you will already know quite a lot about your chosen area, which will help you settle down more quickly. If you are already employed, you become more valuable to your employer.

Your BTEC course will prepare you for the work you want to do.

There are four types of BTEC Level 3 National qualification: Certificates, Subsidiary Diplomas, Diplomas and Extended Diplomas

	Certificate	Subsidiary Diploma	Diploma	Extended Diploma
Credit	30	60	120	180
Equivalence	1 AS level	1 A level	2 A levels	3 A levels

These qualifications are often described as **nested**. This means that they fit inside each other (rather like Russian dolls) because the same units are common to each qualification – so you can progress from one to another easily by completing more units.

TOP TIP

The structure of BTEC Level 3 National qualifications means it's easy to progress from one type to another and gain more credits, as well as to specialise in particular areas that interest you.

- Every BTEC Level 3 National qualification has a set number of **mandatory units** that all learners must complete.
- All BTEC Level 3 National qualifications include **optional units** that enable you to study particular areas in more depth.

- Some BTEC Level 3 National qualifications have **specialist pathways**, which may have additional mandatory units. These specialist pathways allow you to follow your career aims more precisely. For example, if you are studying to become an IT practitioner, you can choose pathways in software development, networking, systems support or IT and business.

- On all BTEC courses you are expected to be responsible for your own learning. Obviously your tutor will give you help and guidance when necessary but you also need to be 'self-starting' and able to use your own initiative. Ideally, you can also assess how well you are doing and make improvements when necessary.

- BTEC Level 3 National grades convert to UCAS points, just like A levels, but the way you are assessed and graded on a BTEC course is different, as you will see in the next section.

Key points

- You can study part-time or full-time for your BTEC Level 3 National.
- You can do a Certificate, Subsidiary Diploma, Diploma or Extended Diploma, and progress easily from one to the other.
- You will study both mandatory units and optional units on your course.
- When you have completed your BTEC course you can get a job (or **apprenticeship**), use your qualification to develop your career and/or continue studying to degree level.
- On all BTEC Level 3 National courses, the majority of your learning is practical and vocationally focused to develop the skills you need for your chosen career.

Using the Edexcel website to find out about your course

- You can check all the details about your BTEC Level 3 National course on the Edexcel website – go to www.edexcel.com.
- Enter the title of your BTEC Level 3 National qualification in the qualifications finder.
- Now find the specification in the list of documents. This is a long document so don't try to print it. Instead, look at the information on the units you will be studying to see the main topics you will cover.
- Then save the document or bookmark the page so that you can easily refer to it again if you need to.

Action points

1 By discussing with your tutor and by exploring the Edexcel website, find out the key information about your course and use it to complete the 'Important information' form on the next page. You can refer to this form at any time to refresh your memory about any part of your studies.

a) Check whether you are studying for a BTEC Level 3 Certificate, Subsidiary Diploma, Diploma, or Extended Diploma, and find out the number of units you will be studying.

b) Find out the titles of the mandatory units you will be studying.

c) Find out the titles of the optional units and identify the ones offered at your centre.

d) Check the length of your course, and when you will be studying each unit.

e) Identify the optional units you will be taking. On some National courses you will do this at the start, while on others you may make your final decision later.

f) Find out other relevant information about your BTEC Level 3 National qualification. Your centre may have already given you details about the course structure.

g) Ask your tutor to help you to complete section 10 on the form. Depending on your course, you may be developing specific additional or personal skills – such as personal, learning and thinking skills (PLTS) and functional skills – or spending time on work experience, going on visits or doing other activities linked to your subject area.

h) Talk to your tutor about section 12 on the form as your sources of information will depend on the careers guidance and information at your centre. You may find it useful to exchange ideas with other members of your class.

IMPORTANT INFORMATION ON MY BTEC LEVEL 3 NATIONAL COURSE	
1	The title of the BTEC Level 3 National qualification I am studying is:
2	The length of my course is:
3	The total number of units I will study is:
4	The number of mandatory units I have to study is:
5	The titles of these mandatory units and the dates (or terms) when I will study them are:
6	The main topics I will learn in each mandatory unit include:

	IMPORTANT INFORMATION ON MY BTEC LEVEL 3 NATIONAL COURSE
7	The number of optional units I have to study is:
8	The titles of the optional units I will study are:
9	The main topics I will learn in each optional unit include:
10	Other important aspects of my course are:
11	After I have achieved my BTEC Level 3 National my options include:
12	Useful sources of information I can use to find out more about these options include:

2 Many learners already have information, contacts or direct experiences that relate to their course. For example, you may have a specific interest or hobby that links to a unit, such as being a St John Ambulance cadet if you are studying Public Services. Think about the relevant sources of information you already have access to and complete the table below.

MY INFORMATION SOURCES	
Experts I know	(Who they are, what they know)
My hobbies and interests	(What they are, what they involve)
My job(s)	(Past and present work and work experience, and what I did)
Programmes I like to watch	(What these are, how they relate to my course)
Magazines and/or books I read	(What these are, examples of relevant articles)
ICT sources	(My centre's intranet as well as useful websites)
Other	(Other sources relevant for my particular course and the topics I will be studying)

Activity: Your future options

At the beginning of a new course it is helpful to think about what options may be available to you for your career pathway in the travel and tourism industry. All assignments and work experience on the programme contribute to your final grade, and knowing what you are aiming for will help keep you motivated.

Using a mind map to explore different ideas is a way for you to start to consider the range of options available to you and what you will need to follow each career pathway.

For example, if you wish to work with people on holiday, you could explore the different routes to becoming a holiday representative.

Becoming a holiday representative is just one of the routes you could follow after your BTEC Level 3 National in Travel and Tourism.

You will find the internet a useful source of information. A good starting point is the website of Tui Travel Plc. Go to page 94 for details of how to access this website.

Use the space on the following page to record your ideas.

Career options available to me in travel and tourism

Step Two: Understand how you are assessed and graded

Case study: Tracking your progress

Richard finds exams hard – no matter how well he prepares, he finds that his mind just seems to go blank when he turns over the exam paper. What Richard likes about the BTEC National in Travel and Tourism is that there are no exams: for each unit he is awarded a pass, merit or distinction. Richard feels more in control of his assessments, as he knows that he will be awarded points for each pass, merit and distinction he achieves.

At the beginning of his BTEC course, Richard's tutors set up a spreadsheet on the VLE so that learners can track their progress. Each time he achieves a pass, merit or distinction grade for a unit, Richard updates his spreadsheet and the relevant points are added. He has a target grade to work towards, and he can see his qualification taking shape. This gives him the impetus he needs to work hard.

As with any qualification, Richard finds that there are some topics he enjoys more than others. He's a sociable guy and he likes the people-focused units such as Customer Service, and all the units associated with holiday destinations and travel. He finds it easy to

aim high in those units, achieving merit and distinction grades. He finds some units like Business of Travel and Tourism harder and a little dry but, with good developmental feedback from his tutors, he finds that he can go back to improve his work. This enables him to achieve higher than pass grades also in some of the units he finds more difficult.

At the end of the first year of his qualification, Richard takes stock of his progress and discusses his final target grade with his tutor. His thoughts by now have turned to going to university to study travel and tourism management or event management, so he is able to see how many UCAS points he needs to progress and how they relate to his BTEC points. Richard is confident that if he continues to aim high in the second year units he will comfortably exceed his target grade.

Reflection points

How will you manage your progress on the course?

Your assessment

This section looks at the importance of your assignments, how they are graded and how this converts into unit points and UCAS points. Unlike A levels, there are no externally-set final exams on a BTEC course. Even if you know this because you already have a BTEC First qualification, you should still read this section as now you will be working at a different level.

Your learning is assessed by **assignments**, set by your tutors. You will complete these throughout

your course, using many different **assessment methods**, such as real-life case studies, **projects** and presentations. Some assignments may be work-based or **time-constrained** – it depends very much on the vocational area you are studying.

Your assignments are based on **learning outcomes** set by Edexcel. These are listed for each unit in your course specification. You must achieve **all** the learning outcomes in order to pass each unit.

TOP TIP

Check the learning outcomes for each unit by referring to the course specification – go to www.edexcel.com.

Important skills to help you achieve your grades include:

*   researching and analysing information (see page 61)
*   using your time effectively (see page 25)
*   working co-operatively as a member of a team (see page 55.)

Your grades, unit points and UCAS points

On a BTEC Level 3 National course, assessments that meet the learning outcomes are graded as pass, merit or distinction. The different grades within each unit are set out by Edexcel as **grading criteria** in a **grading grid**. These criteria identify the **higher-level skills** you must demonstrate

to achieve a higher grade (see also Step Six: Understand your assessment, on page 35).

All your assessment grades earn **unit points**. The total points you get for all your units determines your final qualification grade(s) – pass, merit or distinction. You get:

*   one final grade if you are taking a Certificate or Subsidiary Diploma
*   two final grades if you are taking a Diploma
*   three final grades if you are taking an Extended Diploma.

Your points and overall grade(s) convert to **UCAS points**, which you need to be accepted onto a degree course. For example, if you achieve three final pass grades for your BTEC Level 3 Extended Diploma, you get 120 UCAS Tariff points. If you achieve three final distinction grades, this increases to 360 – equivalent to three GCE A levels.

Please note that all UCAS information was correct at the time of going to print, but we would advise that you check the UCAS website for the most up-to-date information. See page 94 for how to access their website.

Case study: Securing a university place

Chris and Shaheeda both want a university place and have worked hard on their BTEC Level 3 Extended Diploma course.

Chris's final score is 226 unit points, which converts to 280 UCAS Tariff points. Shaheeda has a total score of 228 unit points – just two points more – which converts to 320 UCAS points! This is because a score of between 204

and 227 unit points gives 280 UCAS points, whereas a score of 228 to 251 points gives 320 UCAS points.

Shaheeda is delighted because this increases her chances of getting a place on the degree course she wants. Chris is annoyed. He says if he had realised, he would have worked harder on his last assignment to get two more points.

You start to earn points from your first assessment, so you get many benefits from settling in quickly and doing good work from the start. Understanding how **grade boundaries** work also helps you to focus your efforts to get the best possible final grade.

You will be able to discuss your learning experiences, your personal progress and the

achievement of your learning objectives in **individual tutorials** with your tutor. These enable you to monitor your progress and overcome temporary difficulties. You can also talk about any worries you have. Your tutor is one of your most important resources and a tutorial gives you their undivided attention.

You can talk through any questions or problems in your tutorials.

Key points

- Your learning is assessed in a variety of ways, such as by assignments, projects and real-life case studies.

- You need to demonstrate specific knowledge and skills to achieve the learning outcomes set by Edexcel. You must achieve all the grading criteria to pass a unit.

- The grading criteria for pass, merit and distinction are shown in a grading grid for the unit. Higher-level skills are needed for higher grades.

- The assessment grades of pass, merit and distinction convert to unit points. The total unit points you receive for the course determines your final overall grade(s) and UCAS points.

TOP TIP

It's always tempting to spend longer on work you like doing and are good at, but focusing on improving your weak areas will do more to boost your overall grade(s).

Action points

1 Find out more about your own course by carrying out this activity.

a) Find the learning outcomes for the units you are currently studying. Your tutor may have given you these, or you can find them in your course specification – go to www.edexcel.com.

b) Look at the grading grid for the units and identify the way the requirements change for the higher grades. If there are some unfamiliar words, check these in Step Six of this guide (see page 35 onwards).

c) If the unit points system still seems complicated, ask your tutor to explain it.

d) Check the UCAS points you would need for the course or university which interests you.

e) Design a form you can use to record the unit points you earn throughout your course. Keep this up to date. Regularly check how your points relate to your overall grade(s), based on the grade boundaries for your qualification. Your tutor can give you this information or you can check it yourself in the course specification.

Activity: Understanding grading criteria

When producing assignments it is very important to understand the differences between pass, merit and distinction criteria. Look at the extracts below, taken from examples of work for Unit 25: Handling Air Passengers, and match them up with the possible criteria of P3, M1 or D1.

Example 1

Passenger check-in staff should provide a friendly, speedy and professional service at check-in so that passengers don't have to queue for too long. The standard of service at check-in is important because it will also impact on the airline's image – bad service would have a negative impact. It is important that check-in staff make sure that passengers don't exceed their baggage allowance, because there could be safety implications if baggage exceeded the limits for that aircraft. The questions asked by check-in staff are important because they make the passenger confirm that they have not packed any forbidden objects into their baggage. If a bag was then security-screened and found to have suspect items inside, the passenger would not be able to claim that someone else must have planted the objects into their baggage.

Which criterion does this provide partial evidence for? Why?

Example 2

The check-in staff will check the passengers' tickets and passports against the names on the computer system, weigh and check-in their baggage, and ask security questions. They will allocate seats and give the passengers their boarding passes if the passengers have not already done this online, and also advise them of the expected time of boarding and gate number.

Which criterion does this provide partial evidence for? Why?

Example 3

Manchester Airport's passenger check-in agents have a number of security responsibilities to help ensure safety on board the aircraft. When passengers check in for their flight, the check-in staff ask security questions such as, 'Did you pack this bag yourself?' and 'Has your luggage been left unattended?' As a further security measure, they ask passengers to confirm that they have not packed prohibited items.

Which criterion does his provide partial evidence for? Why?

Step Three: Understand yourself

Case study: Personal qualities

Freya has enjoyed many holidays with her family, both at home and overseas. She loves everything about travel – the hustle and bustle of stations and airports, sitting back and enjoying the journey, exploring different destinations and taking in new experiences. It's this love of travelling that has inspired her to apply for a BTEC Level 3 National course in Travel and Tourism.

Freya is often in awe of the various personnel she meets on her travels – they always seem so confident and self-assured. She would love to be like that but is fairly shy and unsure of her ability. Freya has lots of friends at school and is popular with her peers, but feels that this is because she has grown up with her friends and they know her. It is quite different with strangers, and she is nervous about starting her travel and tourism course in case everyone else is outgoing and brimming with confidence.

Freya talks over her concerns with her careers teacher, who helps her to put things into perspective. The teacher asks her to talk about some of the job roles that interest her in travel and tourism. Together they look at the roles of travel agent, cabin crew and holiday representative, and use job descriptions to identify some of the personal qualities required to carry out these roles effectively. To her surprise Freya finds that many of the key qualities that are needed for these roles are ones that she possesses, such as being reliable, hard-working and friendly.

Freya's teacher explains that confidence develops over time and that even the most outgoing people can suffer from lack of confidence – in fact, their 'big' personalities are often a front that can hide insecurities. Freya now feels more confident about starting her course. She realises that she may need to step outside her comfort zone to tackle certain situations for the first time, but as she becomes more familiar with the course her confidence will increase, just as it will when she eventually starts working in the travel and tourism sector.

Reflection point

How do you think your personality is suited to the BTEC Level 3 Travel and Tourism course you are studying?

Self-awareness means understanding how you 'tick'. For example, do you prefer practical activities rather than theory? Do you prefer to draw or sketch an idea, rather than write about it?

Self-awareness is important as it makes you less reliant on other people's opinions and gives you confidence in your own judgement. You can also reflect on your actions to learn from your experiences.

Self-awareness also means knowing your own strengths and weaknesses. Knowing your strengths enables you to feel positive and confident about yourself and your abilities. Knowing your weaknesses means you know the areas you need to develop.

You can analyse yourself by looking at...

... your personality and preferences

You may have taken a personality test at your centre. If not, your tutor may recommend one to use, or there are many available online.

Many employers ask job candidates to complete a personality test so that they can match the type of work they are offering to the most suitable people. Although these tests can only give a broad indication of someone's personality they may help to avoid mismatches, such as hiring someone who is introverted to work in sales.

... your skills and abilities

To succeed in your assignments, and to progress in a career, requires a number of skills. Some may be vocationally specific, or professional, skills that you can improve during your course – such as sporting performance on a Sports course. Others are broader skills that are invaluable no matter what you are studying – such as communicating clearly and co-operating with others.

You will work faster and more accurately, and have greater confidence, if you are skilled and proficient. A quick skills check will identify any problem areas.

TOP TIP

Use the Skills building section on page 83 to identify the skills you need for your course. You'll also find hints and tips for improving any weak areas.

Key points

- You need certain skills and abilities to get the most out of your BTEC Level 3 National course and to develop your career potential.
- Knowing your strengths and weaknesses is a sign of maturity. It gives you greater confidence in your abilities and enables you to focus on areas for improvement.

TOP TIP

You will find more help in this guide on developing your skills in using time wisely (Step Four), working as a member of a group (Step Seven), researching and analysing information (Step Eight) and making effective presentations (Step Nine).

Action points

1 Gain insight into your own personality by ticking **True** or **False** against each of the following statements. Be honest!

		True	False
a)	If someone annoys me, I can tell them about it without causing offence.		
b)	If someone is talking, I often interrupt them to give them my opinion.		
c)	I get really stressed if I'm under pressure.		
d)	I can sometimes become very emotional and upset on other people's behalf.		
e)	I sometimes worry that I can't cope and may make a mess of something.		
f)	I am usually keen, enthusiastic and motivated to do well.		
g)	I enjoy planning and organising my work.		
h)	I find it easy to work and co-operate with other people and take account of their opinions.		
i)	I am easily influenced by other people.		
j)	I often jump to conclusions and judge people and situations on first impressions.		
k)	I prefer to rely on facts and experience rather than following my instincts.		

Now identify which of the skills and qualities in the box below will be really important in your chosen career.

> tact   truthfulness   listening skills
>
> staying calm under pressure
>
> empathy with others   self-confidence
>
> initiative   planning and organising
>
> working with others   self-assurance
>
> objective judgements

Use your answers to identify areas you should work on to be successful in the future.

2 As part of the UCAS process, all **higher education** applicants have to write a personal statement. This is different from a CV, which is a summary of achievements that all job applicants prepare. You may have already prepared a CV but not thought about a personal statement. Now is your chance!

Read the information about personal statement in the box. Then answer these questions:

a) Explain why personal statements are so important for higher education applicants.

b) Why do you think it is important for your personal statement to read well and be error-free?

c) Suggest three reasons why you shouldn't copy a pre-written statement you have found online.

d) Check websites with information about personal statements to see what to include in the statement and how to set it out.

e) Prepare a bullet point list of ten personal facts. Focus on your strengths and good reasons why you should be given a place on the higher education course of your choice. If possible, discuss your list with your tutor. Then keep it safe, as it will be useful if you need to write a personal statement later.

Personal statements

This is the information that all higher education applicants have to put in the blank space on their UCAS form. The aim is to sell yourself to admissions tutors. It can be pretty scary, especially if you haven't written anything like it before.

So, where do you start?

First, **never** copy pre-written statements you find online. These are just for guidance. Even worse are websites that offer to write your statement for a fee, and send you a few general, pre-written paragraphs. Forget them all: you can do better!

Imagine you are an admissions tutor with 60 places to offer to 200 applicants. What will you need to read in a personal statement to persuade you to offer the applicant a place?

Most likely, clear explanations about:
- what the applicant can contribute to the course
- why the applicant really wants a place on your course
- what the applicant has done to further his/her own interests in this area, such as voluntary work
- attributes that show this applicant would be a definite bonus – such as innovative ideas, with evidence eg 'I organised a newsletter which we published every three months …'

A personal statement should be well written, with no grammatical or spelling errors, and organised into clear paragraphs.

For further guidance on personal statements, go to page 94 to find out how to access a number of helpful websites.

Activity: Preparing your personal statement

On completion of his BTEC National in Travel and Tourism, Jack hopes to progress to university to study business management with travel and tourism. He has prepared a bullet-point list of ten personal facts to include in his personal statement.

Jack's tutor is not very impressed with the lack of detail. He returns the list to Jack and asks for more detail. What general suggestions would you give Jack for how he can expand each of these points?

Ten personal facts	Suggestions for improvement
I have worked hard at college	
I have passed all my year one units	
I spent two weeks' work experience during year one of my course	
I work well as part of a team	
I love travelling	
I enjoy playing sports	
I like socialising	
I have a part-time job	
I want to travel the world	
I want to be a manager	

Step Four: Use your time wisely

Case study: Organising your time

Lee and Jo's class is visiting York as part of their studies for Unit 3: The UK as a Destination. While they are there they have to find out about the features and facilities that attract visitors from the UK and abroad to the city.

Learners have been allowed to divide into groups of three for the visit, and they have to decide on how best to spend their time. Some time has been set aside in class to carry out research and preparation for the visit.

Lee teams up with Shelley and Jade. Lee knows York quite well, so convinces the others that they don't need to do much work. They spend their time in class chatting to one another and their friends on Facebook. During the visit they have a great day, having found some good places to shop and chill. They walk around York but they waste a lot of time as they keep getting lost.

Jo forms a team with Ranie and Ben. They plan for their trip by downloading a map of York, and they prepare a simple worksheet listing the range of facilities and features they have to research for their assignment. They read up about some of these prior to the trip. They also design a simple questionnaire to find out what attracts visitors to York. When they arrive in York they visit the tourist information office to collect leaflets and talk to the staff about different types of visitors. They do a walking tour to see the main attractions, take photographs, and complete their worksheets. They also carry out some primary research, and are able to find both visitors from both the UK and abroad who are happy to answer their questions.

Back at school the teams have to prepare a presentation to describe the features and facilities that attract inbound and domestic visitors to York. Jo and her team do a great job, easily covering the assessment requirements. In contrast, Lee and his team have gathered little tangible evidence – their presentation is superficial, is made up of general internet downloads, and does not meet the grading criteria. They now have to start all over again, and will have to find time for research at the same time as keeping up with new assignments and deadlines.

Reflection point

Are you more like Lee or Jo when managing your time? In what ways?

Most learners have to combine course commitments with other responsibilities such as a job (either full-time or part-time) and family responsibilities. You will also want to see your friends and keep up your hobbies and interests. Juggling these successfully means you need to be able to use your time wisely.

This involves planning what to do and when to do it to prevent panics about unexpected deadlines. As your course progresses, this becomes even more important as your workload may increase towards the end of a term. In some cases, there could be two or more assignments to complete simultaneously. Although tutors try to avoid clashes of this sort, it is sometimes inevitable.

TOP TIPS

When researching for assignments produce a checklist of all the information you have to gather. It will help you to remain focused and on task.

To cope successfully, you need time-management skills, in particular:

- how to organise your time to be more productive
- how to prioritise tasks
- how to overcome time-wasters.

Organising your time

- **Use a diary or wall chart.**
  Using a different colour pen for each, enter:
  - your course commitments, such as assignment dates, tutorials, visits
  - important personal commitments, such as sports matches, family birthdays
  - your work commitments.

TOP TIP

A diary is useful because you can update it as you go, but a wall chart gives you a better overview of your commitments over several weeks. Always keep your diary or chart up to date, and check ahead regularly so that you have prior warning of important dates.

- **Identify how you currently use your time.**
  - Work out how much time you spend at your centre, at work, at home and on social activities.
  - Identify which commitments are vital and which are optional, so you can find extra time if necessary.
- **Plan and schedule future commitments.**
  - Write down any appointments and tasks you must do.
  - Enter assignment review dates and final deadline dates in different colours.
  - This should stop you from arranging a dental appointment on the same morning that you are due to give an important presentation – or planning a hectic social life when you have lots of course work to do.

- **Decide your best times for doing course work.**
  - Expect to do most of your course work in your own time.
  - Work at the time of day when you feel at your best.
  - Work regularly, and in relatively short bursts, rather than once or twice a week for very long stretches.
  - If you're a night owl, allow an hour to 'switch off' before you go to bed.
- **Decide where to work.**
  - Choose somewhere you can concentrate without interruption.
  - Make sure there is space for resources you use, such as books or specialist equipment.
  - You also need good lighting and a good – but not too comfortable – chair.
  - If you can't find suitable space at home, check out your local or college library.
- **Assemble the items you need.**
  - Book ahead to get specific books, journals or DVDs from the library.
  - Ensure you have your notes, handouts and assignment brief with you.
  - Use sticky notes to mark important pages in textbooks or folders.

TOP TIP

Set yourself a target when you start work, so that you feel positive and productive at the end. Always try to end a session when a task is going well, rather than when you are stuck. Then you will be keener to go back to it the next day. Note down outstanding tasks you need to continue with next time.

- **Plan ahead.**
  - If anything is unclear about an assignment, ask your tutor for an explanation as soon as you can.
  - Break down assignments into manageable chunks, such as find information, decide what to use, create a plan for finished work, write rough draft of first section etc.
  - Work back from deadline dates so that you allow plenty of time to do the work.
  - Always allow more time than you need. It is better to finish early than to run out of time.

TOP TIP

If you are working on a task as a group, organise and agree times to work together. Make sure you have somewhere to meet where you can work without disturbing other courses or groups.

- **Be self-disciplined.**
  - Don't put things off because you're not in the mood. Make it easier by doing simple tasks first to get a sense of achievement. Then move on to something harder.
  - Plan regular breaks. If you're working hard, you need a change of activity to recharge your batteries.
  - If you have a serious problem or personal crisis, talk to your personal tutor promptly.

TOP TIP

Make sure you know the consequences of missing an assignment deadline, as well as the dispensations and exemptions that can be given if you have an unavoidable and serious problem, such as illness (see also page 36).

How to prioritise tasks

Prioritising means doing the most important and urgent task first. Normally this will be the task or assignment with the closest deadline or the one that will most affect your overall course grades.

One way of prioritising is to group tasks into ABC categories.

Category A tasks	These must be done now as they are very important and cannot be delayed, such as completing an assignment to be handed in tomorrow.
Category B tasks	These are jobs you should do if you have time, because otherwise they will rapidly become Category A, such as getting a book that you need for your next assignment.
Category C tasks	These are tasks you should do if you have the time, such as rewriting notes jotted down quickly in a lesson.

Expect to be flexible. For example, if you need to allow time for information to arrive, then send for this first. If you are working in a team, take into account other people's schedules when you are making arrangements.

Avoiding time-wasters

Everyone has days when they don't know where the time has gone. It may be because they were constantly interrupted or because things just kept going wrong. Whatever the reason, the end result is that some jobs don't get done.

If this happens to you regularly, you need to take steps to keep on track. Here are some useful tips.

- **Warn people in advance when you will be working.**
  - Ask them to not interrupt you.
  - If you are in a separate room, shut the door. If someone comes in, make it clear you don't want to talk.
  - If that doesn't work, find somewhere else (or some other time) to work.
- **Switch off your mobile, the television and radio, and your iPod/MP3 player.**
  - Don't respond to, or make, calls or texts.
  - If someone rings your home phone, let voicemail answer or ask them to call back later.
- **Be strict with yourself when you are working online.**
  - Don't check your email until you've finished work.
  - Don't get distracted when searching for information.
  - Keep away from social networking sites.
- **Avoid displacement activities.**
  - These are the normally tedious jobs, such as cleaning your computer screen, that suddenly seem far more attractive than working!

Talking to friends can occupy a lot of time.

TOP TIP

The first step in managing your own time is learning to say 'no' (nicely!) if someone asks you to do something tempting when you should be working.

Key points

- Being in control of your time allows you to balance your commitments according to their importance and means you won't let anyone down.
- Organising yourself and your time involves knowing how you spend your time now, planning when and where it is best to work, scheduling commitments and setting sensible timescales to complete your work.
- Knowing how to prioritise means you will schedule work effectively according to its urgency and importance. You will need self-discipline to follow the schedule you have set for yourself.
- Identifying ways in which you may waste time means you can guard against these to achieve your goals more easily.

TOP TIP

Benefits to managing your own time include being less stressed (because you are not reacting to problems or crises), producing better work and having time for a social life.

Action points

1 Start planning your time properly.

a) Find out how many assignments you will have this term, and when you will get them. Put this information into your diary or planner.

b) Update this with your other commitments for the term – both work/course-related and social. Identify possible clashes and decide how to resolve the problem.

c) Identify one major task or assignment you will do soon. Divide it into manageable chunks and decide how long to allow for each chunk, plus some spare time for any problems. If possible, check your ideas with your tutor before you put them into your planner.

2 How good are you at being responsible for your own learning?

a) Fill in this table. Score yourself out of 5 for each area: where 0 is awful and 5 is excellent. Ask a friend or relative to score you as well. See if you can explain any differences.

	Scoring yourself	Other person's score for you
Being punctual		
Organisational ability		
Tidiness		
Working accurately		
Finding and correcting own mistakes		
Solving problems		
Accepting responsibility		
Working with details		
Planning how to do a job		
Using own initiative		
Thinking up new ideas		
Meeting deadlines		

b) Draw up your own action plan for areas where you need to improve. If possible, talk this through at your next **tutorial** (see page 19).

TOP TIP

Don't waste time doing things that distract you when studying for this course. In a travel business, time costs money.

Activity: Manging your time

Managing your time effectively is an important skill for the travel and tourism sector, and many employers look for evidence of time management skills during the recruitment process.

The following questions appear in an application form for the position of retail travel consultant. Imagine you are applying for this position and draft suitable responses:

Give three examples of strategies you use to manage your time effectively:

1.

2.

3.

Why is effective time management important when working as a retail travel consultant?

Step Five: Utilise all your resources

Case study: Preparing for a visit from an industry professional

As part of Unit 6: Preparing for Employment in Travel and Tourism, Miko will be investigating different jobs. Specifically for P2 he must:

- describe the roles and responsibilities, entry requirements and progression routes for two jobs in travel and tourism.

An ex-student is coming into college to talk to Miko's group about his job as a flight attendant. This is something that interests Miko, and he realises that he could use the talk to support his personal ambitions as well as provide evidence for one job in his assignment.

Miko reads the unit specification and his assignment brief to see what information he needs to research for his assignment, and he uses this to produce a template in preparation for the talk. He breaks it down into the following sections:

Section A

- job title, job role, main duties and responsibilities

Section B

- qualifications, skills, personal qualities, experience required
- other factors

Section C

- opportunities for promotion and progression, training, and further and higher education.

Miko finds that there are a number of different websites containing job descriptions and information about the role of cabin crew, and entry requirements. He is able to add some notes to his template prior to the visit. He cannot find out much about promotion, progression and training, and is unsure what would count as 'other factors'.

He also looks at information in the careers library, but finds that some of the resources are a few years old. They contain detailed information, but he will need to check if the information is still current.

By carrying out some of the research in advance, Miko gains a reasonable insight into the job. His research highlights some differences in the information provided by different websites, so he is able to flag these up to remind him to gain clarification during the talk. He also knows that he will have to make the most of the talk to ensure he is able to plug the gaps in his knowledge, and he checks with his tutor what is meant by 'other factors' to make sure he addresses this fully. He feels well prepared for the talk, and is looking forward to finding out more about the role, warts and all!

Reflection points

What are the pros and cons of the different resources used by Miko?

Can you think of any other resources that you could access if you were having to prepare for the same talk?

Your resources are all the things that can help you to be successful in your BTEC Level 3 National qualification, from your favourite website to your **study buddy** (see page 32) who collects handouts for you if you miss a class.

Your centre will provide essential resources, such as a library with appropriate books and electronic reference sources, the computer network and internet access. You will have to provide basic resources such as pens, pencils and file folders yourself. If you have to buy your own textbooks, look after them carefully so you can sell them on at the end of your course.

Here is a list of resources, with tips for getting the best out of them.

- **Course information**. This includes your course specification, this Study Skills Guide and all information on the Edexcel website relating to your BTEC Level 3 National course. Course information from your centre will include term dates, assignment dates and your timetable. Keep everything safely so you can refer to it whenever you need to clarify something.

- **Course materials**. These include course handouts, printouts, your own notes and textbooks. Put handouts into an A4 folder as soon as you get them. Use a separate folder for each unit you study.

TOP TIP

Filing notes and handouts promptly means they don't get lost, and will stay clean and uncrumpled, and you won't waste time looking for them.

- **Stationery**. You need pens and pencils, a notepad, a hole puncher, a stapler and sets of dividers. Dividers should be clearly labelled to help you store and quickly find notes, printouts and handouts. Your notes should be headed and dated, and those from your own research must also include your source (see Step Eight, page 61 onwards.)

- **People**. Your tutors, specialist staff at college, classmates, your employer and work colleagues, your relatives and friends are all valuable resources. Many will have particular skills or work in the vocational area that you are studying. Talking to other learners can help to clarify issues that there may not have been time to discuss fully in class.

A **study buddy** is another useful resource as they can make notes and collect handouts if you miss a session. (Remember to return the favour when they are away.)

Always be polite when you are asking people for information. Prepare the questions first and remember that you are asking for help, not trying to get them to do the work for you! If you are interviewing someone for an assignment or project, good preparations are vital. (See Step Eight, page 61 onwards.)

If someone who did the course before you offers help, be careful. It is likely the course requirements will have changed. Never be tempted to copy their assignments (or someone else's). This is **plagiarism** – a deadly sin in the educational world (see also Step Six, page 35.)

TOP TIP

A positive attitude, an enquiring mind and the ability to focus on what is important will have a major impact on your final result.

Key points

- Resources help you to achieve your qualification. Find out what resources you have available to you and use them wisely.

- Have your own stationery items.

- Know how to use central facilities and resources such as the library, learning resource centres and your computer network. Always keep to the policy on IT use in your centre.

- People are a key resource – school or college staff, work colleagues, members of your class, friends, family and people who are experts in their field.

Action points

1 a) List the resources you will need to complete your course successfully. Identify which ones will be provided by your school or college, and which you need to supply yourself.

b) Go through your list again and identify the resources you already have (or know how to access) and those you don't.

c) Compare your list with a friend's and decide how to obtain and access the resources you need. Add any items to your list that you forgot.

d) List the items you still need to get and set a target date for doing this.

2 'Study buddy' schemes operate in many centres. Find out if this applies to your own centre and how you can make the best use of it.

In some you can choose your study buddy, in others people are paired up by their tutor.

- Being a study buddy might mean just collecting handouts when the other person is absent, and giving them important news.

- It may also mean studying together and meeting (or keeping contact by phone or email) to exchange ideas and share resources.

With a study buddy you can share resources and stay on top of the course if you're ever away.

Activity: Resources

You are just starting your studies on the BTEC National in Travel and Tourism. One of the first units you will be completing is Unit 3: The UK as a Destination.

You will be using the internet for much of your research. However, your tutor is keen for you to use alternative sources of information. Examine the unit specification and make up a resource list using the grid below:

Library-based resources – eg textbooks, newspapers and magazines, maps and atlases, guidebooks	
Resource	**Information source for....**

People and businesses eg relatives and friends, travel agents for holiday brochures, visits, tourist information centres	
Resource	**Information source for....**

Step Six: Understand your assessment

Case study: Libby's assignment troubles

Libby has just received feedback for her first assignment covering P1 for Unit 2: The Business of Travel and Tourism, and she is not very happy. She put lots of information into her report and it was much more detailed than her friend Zach's, yet Zach achieved P1 and she didn't.

Libby's tutor has given clear feedback indicating where she has missed out important information. The key points are that for P1 she has not:

1 included the importance to the international and UK economies, eg GDP, employment
2 provided examples of inbound, outbound and domestic tourism organisations.

Libby compares her work to Zach's and finds that he has covered these and provided examples, although he has not given very detailed descriptions. Zach does tend to try and get away with the minimum amount of work sometimes, but he points out to Libby that the assignment task did ask for 'a brief description plus an example of each of the topic areas' and that is what he has done.

Libby's tutor has indicated in the feedback that Libby's descriptions were incredibly detailed.

She has praised her on her extensive research, but has recommended that Libby focuses carefully on the tasks to make sure that she does not include more than has been asked for at the expense of missing out essential parts of the assessment.

Libby reviews the assignment brief and the unit specification, and she is able to see that she did in fact miss out certain essential parts of the assessment, and included descriptions and detail that were far in excess of the assessment requirements.

Libby realises that she will need to make sure that she doesn't get carried away in future and that she also covers all of the topics required.

She agrees an action plan with her tutor to complete the missing work, and is soon back on track.

Reflection points

How would you avoid making the mistakes that Libby made?

Being successful on any BTEC Level 3 National course means first understanding what you must do in your assignments – and then doing it.

Your assignments focus on topics you have already covered in class. If you've attended regularly, you should be able to complete them confidently.

However, there are some common pitfalls it's worth thinking about. Here are tips to avoid them:

- Read the instructions (the assignment brief) properly and several times before you start.
- Make sure you understand what you are supposed to do. Ask if anything is unclear.

- Complete every part of a task. If you ignore a question, you can't meet the grading criteria.
- Prepare properly. Do your research or reading before you start. Don't guess the answers.
- Communicate your ideas clearly. You can check this by asking someone who doesn't know the subject to look at your work.
- Only include relevant information. Padding out answers makes it look as if you don't know your subject.
- Do the work earlier rather than later to avoid any last-minute panics.
- Pay attention to advice and feedback that your tutor has given you.

Most learners don't do their best in assessments because of silly mistakes, carelessness and rushed work, rather than through major problems of understanding. Make sure you take the time to plan and understand your assignments.

The assignment 'brief'

This may be longer than its name implies! The assignment brief includes all the instructions for an assignment and several other details, as you can see in the table below.

What will you find in a BTEC Level 3 National assignment brief?	
Content	**Details**
Title	This will link to the unit and learning outcomes
Format/style	Written assignment, presentation, demonstration, etc
Preparation	Read case study, do research, etc
Learning outcomes	These state the knowledge you must demonstrate to obtain a required grade
Grading criterion/ criteria covered	Fo example, P1, M1, D1
Individual/group work	Remember to identify your own contribution in any group work
Feedback	Tutor, peer review
Interim review dates	Dates to see your tutor
Final deadline	Last submission date

Reading and understanding each assignment brief is vital. Ask your tutor if there's anything you don't understand.

Your centre's rules and regulations

Your centre will have several policies and guidelines about assignments, which you need to check carefully. Many, such as those listed below, relate to Edexcel policies and guidelines.

- The procedure to follow if you have a serious problem and can't meet a deadline. An extension may be granted.
- The penalty for missing a deadline without good reason.
- The penalty for copying someone else's work. This is usually severe, so never share your work (or CDs or USB flash drive) with anyone else, and don't borrow theirs.
- **Plagiarism** is also serious misconduct. This means copying someone's work or quoting from books and websites and pretending it is your own work.
- The procedure to follow if you disagree with the grade you are given.

Understanding the question or task

There are two aspects to a question or task. The first is the **command words**, which are described below. The second is the **presentation instructions**, which is what you are asked to do – don't write a report when you should be producing a chart!

Command words, such as 'explain', 'describe', 'analyse', 'evaluate' state how a question must be answered. You may be asked to 'describe' something at pass level, but you will need to do more, perhaps 'analyse' or 'evaluate', to achieve merit or distinction.

Many learners fail to achieve higher grades because they don't realise the difference between these words. Instead of analysing or evaluating they give an explanation instead. Adding more details won't achieve a higher grade – you need to change your whole approach to the answer.

The **grading grid** for each unit of your course gives you the command words, so that you know what to do to achieve a pass, merit or distinction. The tables that follow show you what is usually required when you see a particular command word. These are just examples to guide you as the exact response will depend on the question. If you have any doubts, check with your tutor before you start work.

There are two important points to note.

- A command word, such as 'create' or 'explain' may be repeated in the grading criteria for different grades. In these cases the complexity or range of the task itself increases at the higher grades.
- Command words vary depending on your vocational area. So Art and Design grading grids may use different command words from Applied Science, for example.

TOP TIP

Look at this section again when you get your first assignment and check the command words against these explanations.

To obtain a pass grade

To achieve a pass you must usually demonstrate that you understand the important facts relating to a topic and can state these clearly and as concisely as possible.

Command words for a pass	Meaning
Create (or produce)	Make, invent or construct an item.
Describe	Give a clear, straightforward description that includes all the main points and links these together logically.
Define	Clearly explain what a particular term means and give an example, if appropriate, to show what you mean.
Explain … how/why	Set out in detail the meaning of something, with reasons. It is often helpful to give an example of what you mean. Start with the topic then give the 'how' or 'why'.
Identify	Distinguish and state the main features or basic facts relating to a topic.
Interpret	Define or explain the meaning of something.
Illustrate	Give examples to show what you mean.
List	Provide the information required in a list rather than in continuous writing.
Outline	Write a clear description that includes all the main points but avoid going into too much detail.
Plan (or devise)	Work out and explain how you would carry out a task or activity.
Select (and present) information	Identify relevant information to support the argument you are making and communicate this in an appropriate way.
State	Write a clear and full account.
Undertake	Carry out a specific activity.
Examples:	
Identify the main features on a digital camera.	
Outline the steps to take to carry out research for an assignment.	

To obtain a merit grade

To obtain a merit you must prove that you can apply your knowledge in a specific way.

Command words for a merit	Meaning
Analyse	Identify separate factors, say how they relate to each other and how each one relates to the topic.
Classify	Sort your information into appropriate categories before presenting or explaining it.
Compare and contrast	Identify the main factors that apply in two or more situations and explain the similarities and differences or advantages and disadvantages.
Demonstrate	Provide several relevant examples or appropriate evidence which support the arguments you are making. In some vocational areas this may also mean giving a practical performance.
Discuss	Provide a thoughtful and logical argument to support the case you are making.
Explain (in detail)	Provide details and give reasons and/or evidence to clearly support the argument you are making.
Implement	Put into practice or operation. You may also have to interpret or justify the effect or result.
Interpret	Understand and explain an effect or result.
Justify	Give appropriate reasons to support your opinion or views and show how you arrived at these conclusions.
Relate/report	Give a full account, with reasons.
Research	Carry out a full investigation.
Specify	Provide full details and descriptions of selected items or activities.
Examples:	
Compare and contrast the performance of two different digital cameras.	
Explain in detail the steps to take to research an assignment.	

To obtain a distinction grade

To obtain a distinction you must prove that you can make a reasoned judgement based on appropriate evidence.

Command words for a distinction	Meaning
Analyse	Identify the key factors, show how they are linked and explain the importance and relevance of each.
Assess	Give careful consideration to all the factors or events that apply and identify which are the most important and relevant, with reasons.
Comprehensively explain	Give a very detailed explanation that covers all the relevant points and give reasons for your views or actions.
Critically comment	Give your view after you have considered all the evidence, particularly the importance of both the relevant positive and negative aspects.
Evaluate	Review the information and then bring it together to form a conclusion. Give evidence to support each of your views or statements.
Evaluate critically	Review the information to decide the degree to which something is true, important or valuable. Then assess possible alternatives, taking into account their strengths and weaknesses if they were applied instead. Then give a precise and detailed account to explain your opinion.
Summarise	Identify/review the main, relevant factors and/or arguments so that these are explained in a clear and concise manner.
Examples: Assess ten features commonly found on a digital camera. Analyse your own ability to carry out effective research for an assignment.	

TOP TIP

Check that you understand exactly how you need to demonstrate each of the learning outcomes specified in the assignment.

Responding positively

Assignments enable you to demonstrate what you know and how you can apply it. You should respond positively to the challenge and give it your best shot. Being well organised and having confidence in your own abilities helps too, and this is covered in the next section.

Key points

- Read instructions carefully so that you don't make mistakes that can easily be avoided, such as only doing part of the set task.

- Note the assignment deadline on your planner and any interim review dates. Schedule work around these dates to make the most of reviews with your tutor.

- Check your centre's policies relating to assignments, such as how to obtain an extension or query a final grade.

- Expect command words and/or the complexity of a task to be different at higher grades, because you have to demonstrate higher-level skills.

TOP TIP

All your assignments will relate to topics you have covered and work you have done in class. They're not meant to be a test to catch you out.

Action points

1 Check your ability to differentiate between different types of command words by doing this activity.

   a) Prepare a brief description of your usual lifestyle (pass level).

   b) Describe and justify your current lifestyle (merit level).

   c) Critically evaluate your current lifestyle (distinction level).

It would be a good idea to check that your answer is accurate and appropriate by showing it to your tutor at your next tutorial.

TOP TIP

When presenting evidence for an assessment, think about the person who will be looking through it. Plan your 'pitch' well and make it easy for the assessor to match your evidence against the grading criteria.

Sample assignment

Note about assignments
All learners are different and will approach their assignments in different ways.
The sample assignment that follows shows how one learner answered a brief to achieve pass, merit and distinction level criteria. This learner work shows just one way in which these grading criteria can be evidenced. There are no standard or set answers. If you produce the required evidence for each task, then you will achieve the grading criteria covered by the assignment.

Front sheet

Add your name, date and signature to this front sheet before submitting work.

Add the completion date to your planning diary and leave plenty of time to meet the deadline.

Read your assignment brief carefully to see what types of evidence you are being asked to produce.

Learner name		Assessor name	
Claudia Moore		Mr Raj Kumar	

Date issued	Completion date	Submitted on
1 December 2010	16 February 2011	16 February 2011

Qualification	Unit
BTEC Level 3 Diploma in Travel and Tourism	Unit 4: Customer Service in Travel and Tourism

Assignment title	Delivering excellence

In this assessment you will have opportunities to provide evidence against the following criteria. Indicate the page numbers where the evidence can be found.

Criteria reference	To achieve the criteria the evidence must show that the learner is able to:	Task no.	Evidence
P3	describe the customer service skills required to meet customer needs in travel and tourism contexts	1	Learner work 1–3
P4	demonstrate customer service skills in travel and tourism situations	2	Learner work 3–5
M2	deal independently with customers in travel and tourism situations	2	Learner work 3–5
P5	demonstrate selling skills in a travel and tourism situation	3	Observation record page 57
M3	demonstrate effective selling skills in a travel and tourism situation	3	Observation record page 57
D2	demonstrate good product knowledge, customer service and selling skills to provide a consistently high standard of customer service in different situations	2, 3	Observation records pages 54, 56 and 57

Learner declaration

I certify that the work submitted for this assignment is my own and research sources are fully acknowledged.

Learner signature: *Claudia Moore*   Date: *16 February 2011*

These are the criteria that you could achieve by completing this assignment.

You must not copy from other people, or copy extracts from books, the internet or any other sources. Your tutor will explain how to reference sources in your work.

Assignment brief

The scenario puts you into a realistic travel and tourism role and sets the scene for tasks you will carry out in this role.

This is an overview of why you are carrying out this assessment.

You will be provided with a checklist – make sure you cover all parts of this in your work.

Unit title	Unit 4: Customer Service in Travel and Tourism
Qualification	BTEC Level 3 Diploma in Travel and Tourism
Start date	1 December 2010
Interim deadline	3 February 2011
Deadline date	16 February 2011
Assessor	Mr Raj Kumar

Assignment title	Delivering excellence

The purpose of this assignment is to:
enable learners to demonstrate their knowledge and application of customer service and selling skills in travel and tourism situations.

Scenario
You are in your second season as a holiday representative in Palma, Majorca. You look after customers in three large hotels. The main focus of your duties is customer service. This means ensuring your customers enjoy their holiday by giving them information and advice, dealing with problems and complaints and selling excursions and other services, such as car hire. As it is your second season you are also responsible for helping your manager to train new reps.

Task 1
You are to describe the customer service skills required to meet customer needs in the resort. Produce a day's training plan for new reps that describes the customer service skills they will require in order to meet the needs of their customers. This must include a description and relevant examples of communication skills, presentation, teamwork, business skills, complaint handling and selling skills. (See checklist for full details of content to be included.)

This provides evidence towards P3

Task 2a
A customer, Ms Field, comes to find you. Her son, Martin, is with her, with a bandaged foot. He stood on some glass by the swimming pool. He was given first aid by the lifeguard but Ms Field has come to report the incident to you. Although Martin seems fine, she is upset and unhappy about glass lying near the pool. It is a health and safety requirement that drinks are not taken to the pool in glasses or bottles so this should not have happened.

You must deal with the Fields and complete an accident report form (see Appendix page 48). Your assessor may provide an observation record to confirm whether this has been achieved.

This provides evidence towards P4, M2 and D2

Task 2b
You make a check on e-mails at least once a day. You have received an e-mail from Mr Donnelly:

My family was booked on the Sound and Vision excursion yesterday evening. We were supposed to be collected from outside our hotel at 7.30pm. We waited for 45 minutes and the coach did not arrive. Our evening was completely spoilt; we missed the show and had no other plans. My children were very disappointed. I assume you will refund my 300 euros but that is not the point. Our evening was ruined and all because of sloppy organisation on the part of you and your company. I await your urgent reply.

Compose a reply for Mr Donnelly, dealing appropriately with his complaint.

This provides evidence towards P4, M2 and D2

To 'describe' means to write clearly in full sentences to provide information on the listed topics. You can provide descriptive supporting notes to support an outline plan if you prefer.

These are the methods you will use to provide evidence for this assignment.

This shows what you have to do to achieve M2.

These are the methods you will use to provide evidence for this assignment.

Task 2c

All your customers are provided with your mobile phone number. Your phone rings and you receive a query from a customer.

'Hi, we are going home tomorrow night. We are flying from Palma back to Manchester at 8pm but we want to know if you can sort out any help for us at the airport because my wife has hurt her leg. Also we don't know what time we are going to be collected or where from. Can you tell us?'

Respond to the phone call, giving appropriate information and advice. Your assessor may provide an observation record to confirm whether this has been achieved.

This provides evidence towards P4, M2 and D2

You will achieve M2 if you are able to deal independently with the situations in Tasks 2a, 2b and 2c

Task 3

Part of your role is selling excursions to customers on holiday. You present these in a Welcome Meeting but sometimes customers come to you for individual advice. Mr Donnelly, now happy with the result of his complaint to you earlier, would like to go on a full day trip with his family. He is on holiday with his wife and two children. The children are very fair skinned and cannot spend the all day in the sun. The boy is 12 and the girl 10. Mrs Donnelly is very keen on finding out about the local culture and loves shopping too. The children are quite keen to learn about Majorca too but they will easily get bored. Mr Donnelly doesn't mind what they do as long as they are all happy and leave him alone.

You need to research possible excursions in Majorca and then talk to Mr Donnelly and sell him an excursion. Your assessor may provide an observation record to confirm whether this criterion has been achieved. You will need to demonstrate selling skills including building rapport, establishing customer needs and expectations, showing product knowledge including some features and benefits, and demonstrating some skills to overcome objections and close the sale.

This provides evidence towards P5, M3 and D2

You will achieve M3 if you demonstrate effective selling skills, that is, you show that you have product knowledge, can highlight features and benefits, and can close the sale.

You will be awarded D2 where all the tasks in 2 and 3 are carried out to a consistently high standard, demonstrating good product knowledge, selling and customer service skills, demonstrating strong selling skills and excellent product knowledge to bring about a successful sale of suitable products and services to meet customer needs and expectations. When dealing with a complaint, learners will have shown the ability to take control of the situation.

Sources of information

Websites

www.customerservicemanager.com:
community website with news and articles about customer service

http://customerservicezone.com/:
US website with some useful case studies on handling challenging situations

www.majorcaholidays.net:
information on excursions

http://excursions.thomson.co.uk/resort-excursions/000283/Spain/000122/Majorca/000283/Palma-nova.aspx:
information on Thomson Holiday's excursions

This brief has been verified as being fit for purpose			
Assessor	Raj Kumar		
Signature	*Raj Kumar*	Date	*19 November 2010*
Internal verifier	Mr I Worrell		
Signature	*Ian Worrell*	Date	*19 November 2010*

This explains what you have to do to achieve M3.

These are some resources you might find useful. You must reference these and other sources used in your work.

This explains what you have to do to achieve D2.

Use this template to record information during your role play for Task 2a.

Fill in your name here.

You must ask questions as part of the role play to enable you to complete all sections.

Majorca Holidays

Report of an Accident or Dangerous Occurrence

Name of representative making the report:

Property:

Date, time and place where the incident took place. Please be as precise as you can.

Date of incident: Time:

Address where the incident occurred:

Specific location where the incident occurred:

Normal activity carried out at this place:

Reason why the injured person was there:

The injured person
Name:

Booking ref:

Home address:

Nature of injury:

Witnesses
Name:

Address:

Name:

Address:

Describe the incident and how it happened. Draw a sketch if appropriate.

Signed:

NB: Send one copy immediately to the operations manager at HO, one copy to the area manager and one to the person reporting the incident.

Complete all sections neatly, accurately and legibly.

Don't forget to sign it.

Sample learner work

This is an extract of what you will produce. You may either expand the plan to make it descriptive or add supporting notes.

You must include relevant examples to support your description.

Sample learner work: page 1

Task 1: You are to describe the customer service skills required to meet customer needs in the resort (P3).

Produce a day's training plan for new reps which describes the customer service skills they will require in order to meet the needs of their customers. Make sure the plan includes relevant examples. You can make a presentation if you prefer.

Customer service skills for holiday representatives

Training day planned for 6 May 2011

9.15 Registration and welcome	Ensure that uniform is perfect, demonstrating importance of presentation. Ensure training room is clean, tidy and laid out properly with essential resources.
9.30 Introductions and programme for the day	Think about body language and eye contact. Make sure a warm welcome is given demonstrating 'building rapport'.
9.40	**Presentation** Explain the importance of smart appearance, personal hygiene and good grooming. Point out the uniform items and what is to be worn when – casual dress for daytime, suit for evening and excursions. Relate to company image and professionalism. Talk about giving service with a smile and keeping work area clean and tidy. When meeting customers in reception areas, ensure documentation is kept organised and tidy.
10.00	**Communication skills** Explain the different situations a rep works in. Face to face – at the airport, welcome meetings, on tours, meeting times in hotel reception, anywhere you might meet customers, e.g. beach. Always smile, call the customer by name if possible, practise listening skills and use open questioning to develop dialogue. Watch non-verbal communication, so – stand up straight, make eye contact, show that you are listening by nodding, etc. Speak clearly and do not use slang or swear. Telephone – all customers have our number, talk about answering the phone professionally and stating name, smile and listen carefully to the customer's needs. Activities – to show the importance of using questioning and listening skills when dealing with queries and complaints. Written communication – mainly e-mail, letters will be sent by head office but also importance of accurate completion of reports so that they are legible and contain all relevant factual information. Go through structure of an e-mail and language to use according to company policy. Each person to write an e-mail to another. Talk about communication via noticeboard – notices must be checked by another rep for spelling and grammar. Must be neat and clear.
11.00	Coffee.

You can choose to make a presentation if you wish. Make sure it contains full descriptions and examples.

You will carry out some practical activities too.

These are the key topics you must include. Use your checklist to make sure you include everything you need to.

You will carry out some practical activities too

These are the key topics you must include. Use your checklist to make sure you include everything you need to.

Sample learner work: page 2

11.15	**Teamwork** Start with discussion about motivation – what motivates them to work for the company? Go onto what motivates the teams: bonuses, staff awards, possibility of promotion. Show organisation chart and describe the team roles, i.e. manager of resort (Palma) our team manager (5 hotels) our team – 4 reps, 2 children's reps and 1 airport rep. Explain lines of authority and relation to head office. Explore benefits of good teamwork i.e. positive company image, happy staff team, efficient service for customers.
12.15	**Documents** In this session bring examples of company documents. Explain the use of each one and importance of completing each one correctly to avoid errors. Arrivals spreadsheet – check carefully to know who is coming and check against airport rep's sheet. Risk assessment form – to be checked weekly by one of the team at each property. Excursion booking form – make sure all details are completed and payment taken. Record of payments form to record all moneys paid out, collected and deposited with the office. Complaints form. Accidents form. Practise completing the forms – very important to complete factually for every complaint, incident or accident. Must be detailed in case of further action. Contacting HO – explain how to e-mail and how to use the company intranet.
1.00	Lunch.
2.00	**The stages of a sale** Building rapport – ask how we built rapport at the start of the day, explain that you need to get the customer's trust. Establishing customer needs and expectations – it is our job to sell excursions, when selling on an individual basis ask open questions to find out what the customer wants, listen carefully to answers. Product knowledge – read all company literature to understand company policy and programme of excursions, you will be expected to go on excursions to learn about them. Features and benefits – describe the features of our excursions and then promote the benefits, e.g. a trip to Sound and Vision is a spectacular show with many acts, it has something for all the family, a meal is included so no dinner to buy that night, the coach picks everyone up so people can drink if they want to. Overcoming objections, e.g. 'it finishes too late' – you will have such a lovely time and you are on holiday so no need to get up early. Closing the sale – look out for when the customer is ready to buy, e.g. asking the total price. Be ready to take payment and efficiently process the sale without rushing the customer.

These are the key topics you must include. Use your checklist to make sure you include everything you need to.

This tells you what you will do for this practical assessment.

Sample learner work: page 3

3.00	**Handling complaints – the process** Listening, questioning – to establish the facts, empathising, e.g. 'I am sorry you are upset' BUT not admitting any liability. Understanding the problem – may mean finding out what happened from a witness, or checking paperwork. Agreeing a solution – knowing when reps are allowed to decide on a solution and when they must contact a manager. Follow up – checking the customer is happy with the outcome. Practical exercises – role play with complaints.
4.00	Questions and farewell.

Task 2a

A customer, Mrs Field, comes to find you. Her son, Martin, is with her, with a bandaged foot. He stood on some glass by the swimming pool. He was given first aid by the lifeguard but Mrs Field has come to report the incident to you. Although Martin seems fine, she is upset and unhappy about glass lying near the pool. It is a health and safety requirement that drinks are not taken to the pool in glasses or bottles so this should not have happened. You must deal with the Fields and complete an accident report form.
Write a brief evaluation of how you dealt with the Fields.

I greeted Mrs Field by name and asked Martin how he was. He told me what had happened. Mrs Field was calm as she now realised that Martin was not badly hurt. I sympathised with Martin's injury without admitting any fault. I explained that it was company policy to keep glasses and bottles at the bar and that it was usually very well kept to, but on this occasion somebody must have left glass. I explained that we should complete a form. Mrs Field said that she understood that this was just an unfortunate accident.

I was a little bit nervous to start with as I didn't know if the customer would be angry, but I think I dealt with this well. I stayed calm and asked the right questions to enable me to complete my report form. I was careful not to admit any guilt but I used customer service skills by empathising with the customer. She seemed satisfied with my response. I would need to make sure the hotel management take action to prevent glass around the pool area. I will make sure I see these customers again after a day or two to make sure they are still okay and enjoying their holiday.

Signed: *Claudia Moore*   Date: *21 June 2010*

You may be asked to evaluate how you performed in the practical assessments.

Always sign and date feedback and self evaluations.

An observation record on its own is usually not complete evidence. You will also include self evaluation, documentation etc as appropriate.

An observation record on its own is usually not complete evidence. You will also include self evaluation, documentation etc as appropriate.

Make sure your handwriting is neat and legible.

Ask questions to make sure you can complete all sections.

Sample learner work: page 4

Accident Report Form (Task 2a)

Majorca Holidays

Report of an Accident or Dangerous Occurrence

Name of representative making the report: *Claudia Moore*

Property: *Oceans Hotel*

Date, time and place where the incident took place. Please be as precise as you can.

Date of incident: *21st June 2010*   Time: *3.15 pm*

Address where the incident occurred: *Oceans Hotel, Palma*

Specific location where the incident occurred: *Swimming Pool, North side*

Normal activity carried out at this place: *Sunbathers are usually lying here at the side of the pool*

Reason why the injured person was there: *Playing at the pool*

The injured person
Name: *Martin Field*   Booking Ref: *8972*

Home address: *15 Claremont Way, Tavistock, Devon*

Nature of injury: *Cut to sole of foot*

Witnesses
Name: *James Gorgan*

Address: *Oceans Hotel (lifeguard)*

Name:
Address:

Describe the incident and how it happened. Draw a sketch if appropriate.
Martin was playing at the side of the pool and took a few steps towards the pool to jump in. He put his foot on the piece of glass and cut it. He was bleeding and was taken to the first aid post by another child. The lifeguard was able to give first aid and bandaged the foot. He thought the cut was not severe enough to require stitching. It was established that Martin had already had a tetanus jab.

Signed: *Claudia Moore*   Date: *21 June 2010*

NB: Send one copy immediately to the operations manager at HO, one copy to the area manager and one to the person reporting the incident.

Keep your report factual. Don't apportion blame.

Always sign and date feedback and self evaluations.

Your tutor will complete an observation record to confirm how you perform in practical activities

An observation record on its own is usually not complete evidence. You will also include self evaluation, documentation etc as appropriate.

This will confirm what was involved eg a presentation, a role play.

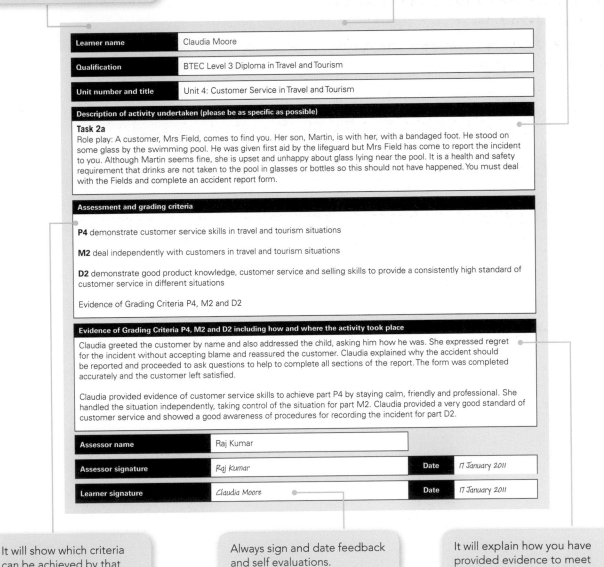

Learner name	Claudia Moore
Qualification	BTEC Level 3 Diploma in Travel and Tourism
Unit number and title	Unit 4: Customer Service in Travel and Tourism

Description of activity undertaken (please be as specific as possible)

Task 2a
Role play: A customer, Mrs Field, comes to find you. Her son, Martin, is with her, with a bandaged foot. He stood on some glass by the swimming pool. He was given first aid by the lifeguard but Mrs Field has come to report the incident to you. Although Martin seems fine, she is upset and unhappy about glass lying near the pool. It is a health and safety requirement that drinks are not taken to the pool in glasses or bottles so this should not have happened. You must deal with the Fields and complete an accident report form.

Assessment and grading criteria

P4 demonstrate customer service skills in travel and tourism situations

M2 deal independently with customers in travel and tourism situations

D2 demonstrate good product knowledge, customer service and selling skills to provide a consistently high standard of customer service in different situations

Evidence of Grading Criteria P4, M2 and D2

Evidence of Grading Criteria P4, M2 and D2 including how and where the activity took place

Claudia greeted the customer by name and also addressed the child, asking him how he was. She expressed regret for the incident without accepting blame and reassured the customer. Claudia explained why the accident should be reported and proceeded to ask questions to help to complete all sections of the report. The form was completed accurately and the customer left satisfied.

Claudia provided evidence of customer service skills to achieve part P4 by staying calm, friendly and professional. She handled the situation independently, taking control of the situation for part M2. Claudia provided a very good standard of customer service and showed a good awareness of procedures for recording the incident for part D2.

Assessor name	Raj Kumar		
Assessor signature	Raj Kumar	Date	17 January 2011
Learner signature	Claudia Moore	Date	17 January 2011

It will show which criteria can be achieved by that activity.

Always sign and date feedback and self evaluations.

It will explain how you have provided evidence to meet certain criteria (or part criteria).

Always use formal language when communicating in writing. Avoid text chat.

Note how to start and finish an email.

Sample learner work: page 5

Task 2b

You make a check on e-mails at least once a day. You have received an e-mail from Mr Donnelly.
'My family was booked on the Sound and Vision excursion yesterday evening. We were supposed to be collected from outside our hotel at 7.30pm. We waited for 45 minutes and the coach did not arrive. Our evening was completely spoilt, we missed the show and had no other plans. My children were very disappointed. I assume you will refund my 300 euros but that is not the point. Our evening was ruined and all because of sloppy organisation on the part of you and your company. I await your urgent reply.'
Compose a reply for Mr Donnelly, dealing appropriately with his complaint.

Dear Mr Donnelly
Thank you for your email. I am so sorry to hear that you missed your excursion. I have checked our paperwork and spoken to our driver. It seems that you are in fact booked on tomorrow evening's Sound and Vision and not yesterday's.

I am not sure how this misunderstanding has occurred but my manager has decided to offer you and your party upgraded seats and a complimentary bottle of champagne at the show to compensate for your spoilt evening. If you would prefer a refund, that can be arranged. Please let me know.

Regards
Claudia

Assessor comment:

Well done Claudia. This is a well written email that acknowledges the customer's complaint, offers an apology and provides a choice of solutions. Good customer service skills have been demonstrated for part P3 and you have worked independently on this for part M2. You have shown a good awareness of options available and your scope of authority. Evidence also supports part achievement of D2. You are doing very well with these situations.

Assessor Signature: *Raj Kumar*   Date: *17 January 2011*

Email responses should be short and to the point.

You may also be asked to evaluate how you handled this.

This will confirm what was involved eg a presentation, a role play.

Learner name	Claudia Moore
Qualification	BTEC Level 3 Diploma in Travel and Tourism
Unit number and title	Unit 4: Customer Service in Travel and Tourism

Description of activity undertaken (please be as specific as possible)

All your customers are provided with your mobile phone number. Your phone rings and you receive a query from a customer.

'Hi, we are going home tomorrow night. We are flying from Palma back to Manchester at 8pm but we want to know if you can sort out any help for us at the airport because my wife has hurt her leg. Also we don't know what time we are going to be collected or where from. Can you tell us?'

Response to phone query from a customer with appropriate information and advice

Assessment and grading criteria

P4 demonstrate customer service skills in travel and tourism situations

M2 deal independently with customers in travel and tourism situations

D2 demonstrate good product knowledge, customer service and selling skills to provide a consistently high standard of customer service in different situations

Evidence is sufficient to support achievement of Grading Criteria P4, M2 and D2

How the activity meets the requirements of the assessment and grading criteria, including how and where the activity took place

Claudia answered the telephone call. I took the part of the customer. The task took place in the classroom.

She was asked about assistance at the airport and to explain how the customer would get to the airport and at what time.

She greeted the customer in a polite and friendly manner. She established the nature of the leg problem and explained about the availability of wheelchairs at the airport. She asked who was in the party and at which hotel. She explained that the coach would arrive at their hotel at 5.30 pm and take them to the airport. They should be ready with their bags packed. She reminded them that liquids could not be taken in hand baggage unless under 100 ml. She reminded them to leave keys at reception. She explained that she would alert the airport representative to make arrangements for wheelchair assistance. Following her explanation she asked if they had any further questions. She wished them a safe journey home and told them if they forgot the time of collection they could look for it on the hotel notice board. Claudia dealt with the enquiry efficiently and independently generating evidence for P4, M2 and D2, demonstrating customer service skills throughout and a good awareness of procedures.

Assessor name	Raj Kumar		
Assessor signature	Raj Kumar	Date	17 January 2011
Learner signature	Claudia Moore	Date	17 January 2011

It will show which criteria can be achieved by that activity.

Always sign and date feedback and self evaluations.

It will explain how you have provided evidence to meet certain criteria (or part criteria).

It will show which criteria can be achieved by that activity.

An observation record on its own is usually not complete evidence. You will also include self evaluation, documentation etc as appropriate.

This will confirm what was involved eg a presentation, a role play.

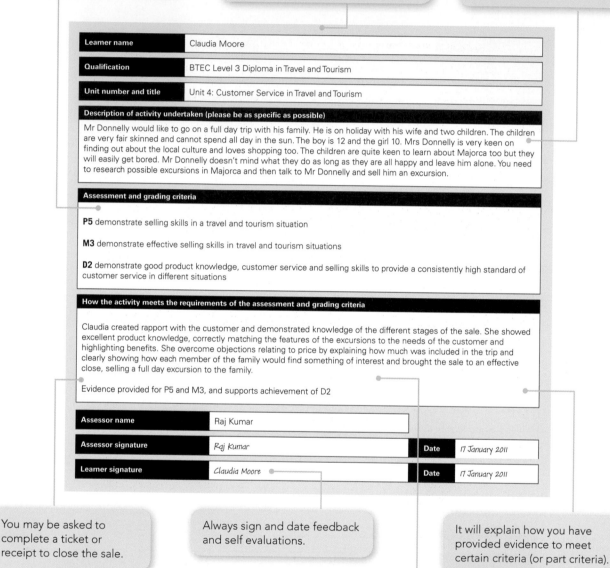

Learner name	Claudia Moore
Qualification	BTEC Level 3 Diploma in Travel and Tourism
Unit number and title	Unit 4: Customer Service in Travel and Tourism

Description of activity undertaken (please be as specific as possible)

Mr Donnelly would like to go on a full day trip with his family. He is on holiday with his wife and two children. The children are very fair skinned and cannot spend all day in the sun. The boy is 12 and the girl 10. Mrs Donnelly is very keen on finding out about the local culture and loves shopping too. The children are quite keen to learn about Majorca too but they will easily get bored. Mr Donnelly doesn't mind what they do as long as they are all happy and leave him alone. You need to research possible excursions in Majorca and then talk to Mr Donnelly and sell him an excursion.

Assessment and grading criteria

P5 demonstrate selling skills in a travel and tourism situation

M3 demonstrate effective selling skills in travel and tourism situations

D2 demonstrate good product knowledge, customer service and selling skills to provide a consistently high standard of customer service in different situations

How the activity meets the requirements of the assessment and grading criteria

Claudia created rapport with the customer and demonstrated knowledge of the different stages of the sale. She showed excellent product knowledge, correctly matching the features of the excursions to the needs of the customer and highlighting benefits. She overcame objections relating to price by explaining how much was included in the trip and clearly showing how each member of the family would find something of interest and brought the sale to an effective close, selling a full day excursion to the family.

Evidence provided for P5 and M3, and supports achievement of D2

Assessor name	Raj Kumar		
Assessor signature	Raj Kumar	Date	17 January 2011
Learner signature	Claudia Moore	Date	17 January 2011

You may be asked to complete a ticket or receipt to close the sale.

Always sign and date feedback and self evaluations.

It will explain how you have provided evidence to meet certain criteria (or part criteria).

You could show visuals from the internet to support your recommendations.

Assessor's comments

You will receive summative feedback to confirm which criteria you have achieved.

Qualification	BTEC Level 3 Diploma in Travel and Tourism	Year	2010–11
Unit number and title	Unit 4: Customer Service in Travel and Tourism	Learner name	Claudia Moore

Grading criteria	Achieved?
P3 describe the customer service skills required to meet customer needs in travel and tourism contexts	Y
P4 demonstrate customer service skills in travel and tourism situations	Y
M2 deal independently with customers in travel and tourism situations	Y
P5 demonstrate selling skills in a travel and tourism situation	Y
M3 demonstrate effective selling skills in a travel and tourism situation	Y
D2 demonstrate good product knowledge, customer service and selling skills to provide a consistently high standard of customer service in different situations	Y

Learner feedback

I liked the practical aspects of this assignment. It was fun role playing with other members of the group and I felt quite relaxed as we had practised a lot before with different situations. It also helped that we had spoken to a holiday rep about her job so we knew about the situations.

Assessor feedback

Well done Claudia. Your training plan covers all the essential skills for P3 and you have successfully related the skills to the role of holiday rep. It would have been even better if you had included your slides with more detail on the different skills required, but you did provide supporting notes to show how you would have developed these areas if you were presenting the training session.

You have demonstrated a consistently high level of customer service in three different situations for P4, including one face to face situation, one written (complaint) and one using the telephone. You also completed an accident form. You always showed politeness and empathy to customers, developed dialogue and listened to what they had to say or reflected carefully on their problems before jumping to a solution.

You showed that you were capable of dealing with these situations effectively and independently to also achieve M2.

For P5 you clearly identified the customer's needs and used independent research so that you had the necessary product knowledge to select and sell the Majorca excursion. You brought the sale to a close and highlighted features and benefits, demonstrating effective selling skills for M3.

Throughout all of the situations you demonstrated good product knowledge and consistently provided a high standard of customer service and selling skills to achieve a positive outcome. Well done. D2 achieved.

Action plan

Your training plan for Task 1 was well thought out. You could have delivered this as a training presentation to help to develop your presentation skills.

Assessor signature	Raj Kumar	Date	18 February 2011
Learner signature	Claudia Moore	Date	20 February 2011

You will have the opportunity to say what you enjoyed/did not enjoy about the assessment

Always sign and date feedback and self evaluations.

You will agree an action plan showing how you could improve your work.

Step Seven: Work productively as a member of a group

Case study: Working successfully in a team

As part of her interview for summer work at a visitor attraction, Shannon is invited to take part in a group interview. One of the tasks is to work as part of a team. The group is divided into teams of eight and they are presented with the hypothetical scenario of a sinking ship. On the ship are a number of famous people, and the teams have to reach agreement on who should be saved and in what order.

Shannon has carried out a similar task at college – she feels very confident and quickly assumes control of the task. Some members of the group are very quiet, but there are a couple of other people who seem to be on Shannon's wavelength, and they become the main decision-makers. Some others do try to make a few suggestions but their contributions are quickly discounted by Shannon.

Shannon and her team complete the task and come up with their list. Shannon checks quickly that everyone is in agreement, and volunteers to act as spokesperson. She feels very pleased with herself as she has managed to get everyone to agree with her list. She hopes she has shown that she is capable of making decisions.

Shannon is disappointed when she doesn't receive an offer of employment. She is surprised to learn from the interviewers that she did not come across as being a good team player and that she was too domineering. She is even more surprised to find that some of the quieter members of the group were in fact offered summer positions.

Reflection points

Do you think it is better to be too dominant or too quiet in group situations?

In your private life, you can choose your own friends, whereas at work you are paid to work alongside many people, whether you like them or not. This applies at school or college too. Hopefully, by now, you've outgrown wanting to only work with your best friends on every project.

You may not be keen on everyone in your team, but you should still be pleasant and co-operative. This may be harder if you are working with a partner than in a large group.

Sometimes you may be the group leader. This may inspire you, or fill you with dread. You won't be expected to develop team-leader skills overnight, but it helps if you know the basics.

First, you should understand how groups and teams work and why good teamwork is considered vital by employers.

Working in groups and teams

If you have a full-time or part-time job, you already belong to a working group, or team. At school or college your class is an example of a working group.

All working groups have some common characteristics:

- doing the same type of work – though in the workplace you probably have different roles or responsibilities
- a group leader or supervisor
- a reason for working together, such as studying for the same qualification or tackling an area of work too large for someone to do alone
- group members are dependent on each other in some way; at work you may have to cover someone's workload if they are absent
- group members concentrate on their individual achievements and success.

A team is different. As a team member you have a specific objective to achieve **together** – and this is more important than the goals of individual team members.

TOP TIP

Understanding how groups and teams function will help you be a better team worker and a better team leader.

These are the characteristics of a team.

- Team members have a team goal which is more important than any personal goals.
- Team members have complementary skills so that the team can achieve more than individuals working alone could achieve.
- Work is allocated to play to each person's strengths and talents.
- The team members give each other encouragement and support.
- There is collective responsibility for achieving the goal.

A good team leader acts as facilitator and motivator, and gives practical support and guidance.

Working in a team has many benefits. Team members can learn from each other and combine their skills to do a better job more quickly. Working with other people is often more enjoyable than working alone, too. Many industries rely heavily on efficient group working, from IT teams to health workers and the emergency services.

TOP TIP

Focusing on the task rather than on personalities is the first step in learning to work with different people, whose views may not match your own.

There are many benefits to be gained from working as a team.

Being a good team member

Everyone wants team members who are talented, positive, cheerful and full of energy. These are the key areas to focus on if you wish to be a good team member.

- **Your social skills.** This includes being courteous, treating other people as you wish to be treated, saying 'please' when you want something and thanking people who do you a favour.

- **Your temperament**. Expect people to have different views and opinions from you and don't take offence if someone disagrees with you. If you lose your temper easily, learn to walk away before you say something you may regret.

- **Your communication skills.** This includes talking and listening!

Practise saying what you mean clearly, accurately and succinctly. Be prepared to give good reasons to justify your arguments and ideas.

Allow people to finish what they're saying, without interruption, before you talk. Never shout people down. Think before you speak so that you don't upset people with tactless remarks. If you inadvertently do so, apologise.

- **Your commitment.** Always keep your promises and never let anyone down when they are depending upon you. Always do your fair share of the work, even if you don't agree with all the decisions made by your team. Tell people promptly if you are having problems so there is time to solve them. Be loyal to your team when you're talking to other people.

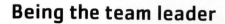

Being the team leader

It can be difficult to strike a balance between 'leading' the team and working with friends. You need to inspire and motivate your team without being bossy or critical.

Important points to remember about being a team leader

- Lead by example. Stay pleasant, consistent and control your temper, even under pressure.

- Everyone is different. Your ways of working may not always be the best.

- Be prepared to listen and contribute positively to a discussion.

- Encourage quieter team members to join in discussions by asking for their views.

- Be prepared to do whatever you ask other people to do.

- Note down what you say you will do, so that you don't forget.

- Discuss alternatives with people rather than giving orders.

- Be sensitive to other people's feelings. They may have personal problems or issues that affect their behaviour.

- Learn the art of persuasion.

- Act as peacemaker. Help people reach a compromise when necessary.

- Give team members the credit for their hard work or good ideas.

- Admit your mistakes. Look for a positive solution and think about what can be learned for the future, rather than making excuses.

- Praise and encourage team members who are working hard.

- Make criticisms constructively, and in private.

- Be assertive (put forward your point of view firmly) rather than aggressive (attacking other people to defend yourself).

Some notes of caution about being a team leader

- Try to look pleasant and don't glare at people who interrupt you unexpectedly.

- Never talk about team members behind their backs.

- Don't gossip, exaggerate to make a point, spread rumours, speculate or tell lies.

- Don't expect to get your own way all the time – all good leaders back down on occasion.

- Never criticise any colleagues in front of other people. Speak to them in private and keep it constructive.

TOP TIP

Excellent ideas often come from quiet team members. Encourage everyone to make suggestions so that you don't overlook any valuable contributions.

Key points

- There are many benefits of working in a group or as a team. These include mutual support, companionship and the exchange of ideas.
- You will be expected to work co-operatively with other people at work, and during many course assignments.

- It isn't easy learning to be a team leader. Team leaders should be fair, consistent and pleasant to work with, as well as loyal and sensitive to the needs of team members.

Action points

1 Identify the role of teamwork in your area of study. Identify the team's goal and any factors you think will contribute towards its success.

2 Decide how you would handle each of the following difficult situations if you were the team leader. If you can, discuss your ideas with a friend in your class.

   a) The team needs to borrow a college video camera to record an event being held tonight. Your tutor tells you that the one you reserved last week is not working and the rest are out on loan.

   b) A member of your team has personal problems so you have given him less work to do. Now you've been accused of having favourites.

   c) A team member is constantly letting everyone down because of poor work and non-attendance at group meetings.

   d) Two team members have disagreed about how to do a task. You're not bothered how they do it as long as it gets done properly, and by the deadline.

   e) A team member becomes very aggressive whenever she is challenged in any way – no matter how mildly.

3 Identify someone who has inspired you because they've been an excellent leader. This could be someone you've met, a fictional character or a famous person. Note down what it is about them that impressed you.

TOP TIP

Team working, and bouncing ideas around, produces quicker and better results than working in isolation. Travel and Tourism businesses actively encourage teamwork.

Activity: Being diplomatic

Your class is completing Unit 23: Residential Study Visit. This will involve planning and taking part in a trip of at least two nights. In the first part of the unit your class has to put forward proposals for a residential study visit, and it seems that the team leader needs a few lessons in how to be more diplomatic.

Here are some of the things she has said in meetings. How could she have re-phrased her comments to be more constructive and get the best out of the team?

What was said...	How it might have been said...
Who in their right mind would be interested in going there?	
You're really lazy - no wonder no-one wants to work with you.	
You always think you know best, don't you?	
What do you mean you can't afford it?	
I cannot imagine anyone wanting to pay for such a boring trip.	
Stop bragging about all the places you've been to.	
I don't care what you think. I'm the team leader so I have the final say.	
You're hopeless. Can't you get anything right?	

Step Eight: Understand how to research and analyse information

Case study: The benefits of good research

Angie is studying unit 11: Investigating the Cruise Industry. She is completing the first assignment to describe the cruise industry environment. Angie is fortunate as her tutor has developed the group's knowledge of the cruise industry by using a variety of delivery methods:

- They have had a talk from a specialist cruise agent who has explained how the cruise industry has developed, particularly over the last 50 years.
- They have read and discussed newspaper articles about new developments in cruising.
- They have watched promotional DVDs produced by different cruise lines.
- They have worked in groups to research and produce a display showing the main cruise lines.
- They have used the internet and cruise brochures to carry out paired research into different cruise ships, and shared their research with the class.
- They have interviewed family members and friends who have taken a cruise as a holiday.

With all of this information available to her Angie feels well prepared for her assignment: to write an article describing the cruise industry environment.

Angie puts a lot of thought into producing her article. She identifies where she needs to carry out additional research, and sources some good photographs to give her article visual appeal. Angie thinks carefully about what to include so that she covers everything but does not waffle.

She is well on target for meeting her deadline and has almost completed the article when disaster strikes. Her pen drive becomes infected with a virus and she loses all her work. Angie has not saved her work elsewhere so there is nothing for it but to start again.

Fortunately, because Angie's knowledge has been built up by carrying out different activities, she has lots of her research notes and materials available to help her to start again. Angie is relieved that her research was so thorough, although this has proved that she should save her work in more than one place in future!

Reflection points

Think about how thorough your research is, and if there are any improvements you should make.

As a BTEC Level 3 National learner, you often have to find information for yourself. This skill will be invaluable in your working life, and if you continue your studies at higher education level. Sometimes the information will give you a better understanding of a topic, at other times you will research information for a project or assignment. Sometimes you may be so interested in something that you want to find out more without being told to do so!

Whatever your reason, and no matter where your information can be found, there is a good and not so good way to go about the task. This section

TOP TIPS

When reading newspapers and magazines or browsing the internet look out for newsworthy stories of what's happening around the world that might impact on travel and tourism.

will help if you can't find what you want, or find too much, or drift aimlessly around a library, or watch a demonstration and don't know what to ask afterwards.

Types of information

There are many types of information and many different sources. Depending on the task, these are the sources you may need to consult.

- **Verbal information.** This includes talking to friends, colleagues at work, members of your family, listening to experts explain what they do, interviewing people, talking to sales reps at an exhibition or customers about a product.

- **Printed information**. This includes information printed in newspapers, journals, magazines, books, posters, workshop manuals, leaflets and catalogues. The type of magazine or newspaper you read may have its own slant on the information, which you may have to take into account (see page 65).

- **Written information**. This includes course notes and handouts, reports and other documents in the workplace. If you want to use written information from work, you must check this is allowed, and that it doesn't contain confidential material such as financial information or staff names and addresses.

- **Graphical information.** This includes illustrations, pictures, cartoons, line drawings, graphs and photographs. Graphics can make something clearer than words alone. For example, a satnav instruction book might contain illustrations to show different procedures.

- **Electronic information.** This includes information from electronic sources such as DVDs, CD-ROMs, searchable databases, websites, podcasts, webinars (**seminars** online), emails and text messages. The huge amount of information available online is both a help and a hindrance. You can find information quickly, but the source may be unreliable, out of date, inaccurate or inappropriate (see page 64.)

TOP TIP

Too much information is as bad as too little, because it's overwhelming. The trick is to find good quality, relevant information and know when to call a halt to your search.

TOP TIP

Consider all appropriate sources and don't just rely on information found online.

Finding what you need

Spend a few minutes planning what to do before you start looking for information. This can save a lot of time later on.

The following steps will help you to do this.

1 Make sure you understand exactly what it is you need to know so that you don't waste time looking for the wrong thing.

2 Clarify your objectives to narrow down your search. Think about why the information is wanted and how much detail you need. For example, learners studying BTEC Nationals in Engineering and Performing Arts may both be researching 'noise' for their projects but they are likely to need different types of information and use it in different ways.

3 Identify your sources and check you know how to use them. You need to choose sources that are most likely to provide information relevant to your objectives. For example, an engineering learner might find information on noise emissions in industry journals and by checking out specialist websites.

4 Plan and schedule your research. Theoretically, you could research information forever. Knowing when to call a halt takes skill. Write a schedule that states when you must stop looking and start sorting the information.

5 Store your information safely in a labelled folder. This folder should include printouts or photocopies of articles, notes about events you have attended or observed, photographs you've taken or sketches you've drawn. Divide your information under topic headings to make it easier to find. When you're ready to start work, re-read your assignment brief and select the items that are most closely related to the task you are doing.

Primary and secondary research, and the law of copyright

There are two ways to research information. One is known as primary research, the other is secondary research.

Primary research

Primary research involves finding new information about an issue or topic. This might include finding out people's views about a product or interviewing an expert. When carrying out interviews, you will need to design a survey or questionnaire. Your primary research might also include observing or experiencing something for yourself, and recording your feelings and observations.

Secondary research

Secondary research involves accessing information that already exists in books, files, newspapers or on CD-ROMs, computer databases or the internet, and assessing it against your objectives.

This information has been prepared by other people and is available to anyone. You can quote from an original work provided you acknowledge the source of your information. You should put this acknowledgement in your text or in the bibliography to your text; do not claim it as your own research. You must include the author's name, year of publication, the title and publisher, or the web address if it is an online article. You should practise listing the sources of articles so

that you feel confident writing a bibliography. Use the guidance sheet issued by your centre to help you. This will illustrate the style your centre recommends. (See also page 67.)

The trick with research is to choose the best technique to achieve your objectives and this may mean using a mix of methods and resources. For example, if you have to comment on an industry event you might go to it, make notes, interview people attending, observe the event (perhaps take a video camera), and read any newspaper reports or online comments.

People as a source of information

If you want to get the most out of interviewing someone, or several people, you need to prepare carefully in advance.

The following points give some general advice about getting the most out of face-to-face interviews.

- Make sure you know what questions to ask to get the information you need.
- Explain why you want the information.
- Don't expect to be told confidential or sensitive information.
- Write clear notes so that you remember who told you what, and when. (See also page 66.)
- Note the contact details of the person you are interviewing and ask whether they mind if you contact them again should you think of anything later or need to clarify your notes.
- Thank them for their help.

If you want to ask a lot of people for their opinion, you may want to conduct a survey. You will need to design a questionnaire and analyse the results. This will be easier if you ask for **quantitative** responses – for example yes/no, true/false or ratings on a five-point scale – rather than opinions.

- Give careful thought to your representative sample (people whose opinions are relevant to the topic).
- Decide how many people to survey so that the results mean something.
- Keep the survey relatively short.
- Thank people who complete it.
- Analyse the results, and write up your conclusions promptly.

TOP TIP

Test your questionnaire on volunteers before you 'go live' to check that there are no mistakes and the questions are easy to understand. Make any amendments before you conduct your 'real' survey.

Asking someone who knows a lot about a topic can be informative.

Avoiding pitfalls

Wikipedia is a good online source that covers many topics, and often in some depth. It is popular and free. However, it has an open-content policy, which means that anyone can contribute to and edit entries. People may post information, whether it is correct or not. Wikipedia is moving towards greater checks on entries, but it is still sensible to check out information you find on this site somewhere else.

Apart from inaccuracy, there are other problems that you may find with any information you obtain through research, especially online material.

- **Out-of-date material.** Check the date of everything and keep only the latest version of books, newspapers or magazines. Yesterday's news may be of little use if you are researching something topical.
- **Irrelevant details.** Often, only part of an article will be relevant to your search. For example, if you are forecasting future trends in an area of work, you do not need information about its history or related problems. When learners are struggling, they sometimes 'pad out' answers with irrelevant information. If you've researched properly you can avoid this by having enough relevant information for your purposes.

- **Invalid assumptions.** This means someone has jumped to the wrong conclusion and made 2 + 2 = 5. You might do this if you see two friends chatting and think they are talking about you – whether they are or not! You can avoid problems in this area by double-checking your ideas and getting evidence to support them.

- **Bias.** This is when people hold strong views about a topic, or let their emotions or prejudices affect their judgement. An obvious example is asking a keen football fan for an objective evaluation of their team's performance!

- **Vested interests.** People may argue in a certain way because it's in their own interests to do so. For example, when the government said Home Information Packs must be prepared for all properties being sold, the Association of Home Information Pack Providers was in favour because it trains the people who prepare the packs. The National Association of Estate Agents and Royal Institution of Chartered Surveyors were not because they thought they would lose business if people were put off selling their houses.

TOP TIP

Don't discard information that is affected by bias or vested interests. Just make it clear you know about the problem and have taken it into account.

Reading for a purpose

You may enjoy reading or you may find it tedious or difficult. If so, it helps to know that there are different ways to read, depending on what you're doing. For example, you wouldn't look for a programme in a TV guide in the same way that you would check an assignment for mistakes. You can save time and find information more easily if you use the best method of reading to suit your purpose. The following are some examples of ways of reading.

- **Skim reading** is used to check new information and get a general overview.
  To skim a book chapter read the first and last paragraphs, the headings, subheadings and illustrations. It also helps to read the first sentence of each paragraph.

TOP TIP

News articles are written with the key points at the beginning, so concentrate on the first paragraph or two. Feature articles have a general introduction and important information is contained in the main text.

- **Scanning** is used to see whether an article contains something you need – such as key words, dates or technical terms.
  Focus on capital or initial letters for a name, and figures for a date. Technical terms may be in bold or italics.

- **Light reading** is usually done for pleasure when you are relaxed, for example, reading a magazine article. You may not remember many facts afterwards, so this sort of reading isn't suitable for learning something or assessing its value.

- **Word-by-word reading (proofreading)** is important so that you don't miss anything, such as the dosage instructions for a strong medicine. You should proofread assignments before you submit them.

- **Reading for study (active reading)** means being actively involved so that you understand the information. It is rare to be naturally good at this, so you might have to work to develop this skill.

Developing critical and analytical skills

Developing critical and analytical skills involves looking at information for any flaws in the arguments. These skills are important when you progress to work or higher education (HE), so it's useful to practise them now on your BTEC Level 3 National course.

A useful technique for understanding, analysing, evaluating and remembering what you are reading is **SQ4R**.

SQ4R is an effective method. It consists of six steps.

1 Survey first, to get a general impression. Scan the information to see what it is about, when it was written and by whom. The source, and the reason it was written, may be important. Most newspapers, for example, have their own 'slant' that affects how information is presented.

2 Question your aims for reading this material. What are you hoping to find? What questions are you expecting it to answer?

3 Read the information three or four times. The first time, aim to get a general idea of the content. Use a dictionary to look up any new words. Then read more carefully to really understand what the writer means.

4 Respond by thinking critically about the information and how it relates to the topic you are studying. Does it answer your queries partially, fully or not at all? What information is factual and what is based on opinion? Is there evidence to support these opinions? Is there a reason why the author has taken this standpoint? Do you agree with it? How does it link to other information you have read? What is the opposite argument and is there any evidence to support this? Overall, how useful is this information?

5 Record the information by noting the key points. Use this to refresh your memory, if necessary, rather than re-reading the article.

6 Review your notes against the original to check you have included all important points. If you are also preparing a presentation, reviewing your notes will help you to remember key points more easily.

TOP TIP

SQ4R is just one method of reading for study. Research others and adapt them to suit your own style.

Taking good notes

There are many occasions when you need to take notes, such as when a visiting speaker is talking to your class. There's no point taking notes unless you write them in a way that will allow you to use them later.

Note-taking is a personal activity. Some people prefer to make diagrammatical sketches with key points in boxes linked by arrows, others prefer to write a series of bullet points. You will develop your own style, but the following hints and tips might help you at the start.

- Use A4 lined paper, rather than a notebook, so that you have more space and don't need to turn over so often.
- When you're reading for study, make sure you have a dictionary, pen, notepad and highlighter to hand.
- Leave a wide margin to record your own comments or queries.
- Put a heading at the top, such as the speaker's name and topic, as well as the date.
- If you are making notes from a book or an article, remember SQ4R and read it several times first. Your notes will only be effective if you understand the information.
- Don't write in complete sentences – it takes too long.
- Leave spaces for later additions or corrections.
- Use headings to keep your notes clear and well organised.
- Only write down relevant information, including key words and phrases.

- Highlight, underline or use capitals for essential points.
- Never copy chunks of text – always use your own words.
- Clearly identify quotations, and record your sources, so that you can cite them in your work. (Note the author's name, title, publisher, date and place of publication and the page number.)

TOP TIP

Make sure your information is accurate, up to date, relevant and valid. Be aware of bias, and don't confuse fact with opinion.

Key points

- Useful information may be verbal, printed, written, graphical or electronic.
- Effective research means knowing exactly what you are trying to find and where to look. Know how reference media are stored in your library and how to search online. Store important information carefully.
- Primary research is original data you obtain yourself. Secondary research is information prepared by someone else. If you use this, you must quote your sources in a bibliography.
- You can search for information by skimming and scanning, and read in different ways. Reading for study means actively involving yourself with the text, questioning what you are reading and making notes to help your own understanding.
- Read widely around a topic to get different viewpoints. Don't accept everything you read as correct. Think about how it fits with other information you have obtained.
- Taking notes is a personal skill that takes time to develop. Start by using A4 lined pages with a margin, set out your notes clearly and label them. Only record essential information.

Action points

- Working with a friend, look back at the sources of information listed on page 62. For each type, identify examples of information relevant to your course that you could obtain from each source. See how many you can list under each type.
- Check your ability to find the information you need by answering each of the questions in **Activity: Finding information** on the next page. For any questions you get wrong, your first research task is to find out the correct answers as quickly as you can.
- Go to page 94 to find out how you can access a website where you can check your ability to skim and scan information, improve your ability to differentiate fact from opinion, summarise text, and much more.
- Check your ability to sort fact from opinion and spot vested interests by completing **Activity: Let's give you a tip...** on page 70. Check your ideas with the answers on page 93.

TOP TIP

Make a note of any information that you are struggling to understand so that you can discuss it with your tutor.

Activity: Finding information

Answer the following questions about finding information.

a) Four types of information that are available from the library in your centre, besides books, are:

1

2

3

4

b) When I visit the library, the way to check if a book I want is available is:

c) The difference between borrowing a book on short-term loan and on long-term loan is:

Short-term loan:

Long-term loan:

d) The journals that are stocked by the library that are relevant to my course include:

e) Useful information on the intranet at my centre includes:

f) Searchable databases and online magazines I can access include:

g) The quickest way to check if a book or journal contains the type of information I need is to:

h) The difference between a search engine, a portal, a directory site and a forum is:

i) Bookmarking useful websites means:

j) In addition to suggesting websites, Google can also provide the following types of information:

k) Specialist websites which provide useful information related to my course include:

l) Useful tips I would give to people starting on my course who need to find out information are:

Activity: Let's give you a tip...

In 2009, many businesses were struggling thanks to the credit crunch and falling consumer demand. Some, like Woolworths, closed down altogether. Others laid off staff, or announced wage cuts. Despite this, the government approved recommendations by the Low Pay Commission to increase the minimum wage rate from October. Although the rise was only small, many unions, including Unison and Usdaw, agreed it was better than a freeze, which had been wanted by the British Chambers of Commerce and the British Retail Consortium.

The government also announced new laws to stop restaurants and bars using tips to top up staff pay to the minimum level. *The Independent* newspaper claimed its 'fair tips, fair pay' campaign had won the day. It also reported that the British Hospitality Association was claiming this could result in up to 45,000 job losses. The Unite union also carried out a campaign and its General Secretary claimed the decision a triumph for the poorly paid. Not everyone agreed. Some thought there should be no tipping at all, as in Australia. Others said the Canadian system was best – wages are low but generous tips are left, and this motivates staff to give excellent service.

a) Look at the table below. In your view, which of the statements are facts and which are opinions? In each case, justify your view.

Statement	Fact or opinion?	Justification
i) Having a national minimum wage helps low-paid workers.		
ii) Over one million people will benefit from the minimum wage increase.		
iii) The new law on tips will stop restaurants paying below minimum wage rates.		
iv) Using the Australian system of no tips would be better.		
v) The Canadian system guarantees good service.		
vi) 45,000 job losses will occur in the hospitality industry.		

b) All newspapers have their own way of putting forward the news. Go to page 94 to find out how to access a website for this page. From here, you can access a website which will help you to compare the way that news is reported in different newspapers.

Compare six different newspapers and make notes on:

i) the type of stories covered

ii) the way views are put forward.

Activity: Carrying out research

As part of your studies you will be investigating developments that have shaped the present-day travel and tourism sector since the 1960s. Not all of the information you research will be based on fact, so you have to be careful to check the reliability of your sources.

The development of space tourism is one of the most exciting subjects of this century, and you decide you would like to find out more about this. Carry out some research to find out about developments in space tourism. Some of the information you research will be factual, but some will be based on opinion or supposition, as no one can really tell at this stage how space tourism will develop.

Carry out some research using at least three websites to find out some information about the development of space tourism.

Website	Summary of findings	Fact or opinion/ supposition?

How easy was it to locate information about space tourism?

_____

_____

How could you check the reliability of your sources?

_____

_____

_____

Step Nine: Make an effective presentation

Case study: Preparing for presentations

Sally is attending an interview for the post of trainee sales representative for a local hotel group. The letter of invitation indicates that the morning session will take the form of a group interview, during which candidates will have to make a presentation on one of the following topics:

- my favourite holiday destination
- my favourite hobby or pastime.

The briefing notes indicate that this will be a timed 90-second presentation, and candidates will be allowed to use visual aids.

Fortunately for Sally she has had plenty of practice at making presentations as part of her BTEC National in Travel and Tourism. She used to panic at the thought of presentations, but has become much more used to them over time.

She decides to make a presentation about a fantastic holiday to Las Vegas. Ninety seconds is not long, so she plans carefully, focusing on the unusual aspects to sell the delights of 'Sin City'. She injects some humour and uses some great photographs in her visual aids.

The time she spends preparing for the presentation is well spent. Her timing is perfect, everything she includes is relevant, and she gets a few laughs. Some of the other presentations are not very well planned, and Sally's stands out as one of the best. It helps to secure her place in the next stage of the selection process.

Reflection points

Think about any particularly memorable presentations you have done previously. What made them stand out?

TOP TIPS

Practice makes perfect. Try recording your presentations and play them back to yourself to identify areas for improvement.

Making a presentation can be nerve-wracking. It involves several skills, including planning, preparation and communication. It tests your ability to work in a team, speak in public and use IT (normally PowerPoint). You also have to stay calm under pressure. However, as it is excellent practice for your future, you can expect presentations to be a common method of assessing your performance.

TOP TIP

When you're giving a presentation, keep to time, get to the point and use your time as well as you can.

Good planning and preparation

Being well prepared, and rehearsing beforehand, helps your confidence and your presentation. The following points will help you to do this.

- If you're part of a team, find out everyone's strengths and weaknesses and divide work fairly taking these into account. Decide how long each person should speak, who should introduce the team and who will summarise at the end.

- Take into account the time you have been allocated, your resources and team skills. A simple, clear presentation is better – and safer – than a complicated one.

- If you're using PowerPoint, make slides more interesting by avoiding a series of bulleted lists and including artwork. Print PowerPoint notes for the audience. Use a fuller set of notes for yourself, as a prompt.

- Check the venue and time.

- Decide what to wear and check it's clean and presentable.

- Prepare, check and print your handouts.

- Decide, as a team, the order in which people will speak, bearing in mind the topic.

- Discuss possible questions and how to answer them.

- Rehearse beforehand to check your timings.

If you prepare properly, you can really enjoy giving a presentation.

TOP TIP

Rehearsing properly allows you to speak fluently, just glancing at your notes to remind you of the next key point.

On the day, you can achieve a better performance if you:

- arrive in plenty of time
- calm your nerves by taking deep breaths before going in front of your audience
- introduce yourself clearly, and smile at the audience
- avoid reading from your screen or your notes
- explain what you are going to do – especially if giving a demonstration – do it and then review what you've done
- say you will deal with questions at the end of any demonstration
- answer questions honestly – don't exaggerate, guess or waffle
- respond positively to all feedback, which should be used to improve your performance next time.

TOP TIPS

Make sure you can be heard clearly by lifting your head and speaking a little more slowly and loudly than normal.

Key points

- When making a presentation, prepare well, don't be too ambitious and have several rehearsals.
- When giving a demonstration, explain first what you are going to do and that you will answer questions at the end.

Case study: Learner quotes about making presentations

Most people start off feeling uncomfortable about talking in front of a group of people, whether you know them or not. This is what some real learners have said about having to give presentations as part of their BTEC course.

"I actually feel more comfortable giving a presentation rather than having to write an essay. What I really enjoy about it is the fact that sometimes we have to prepare a presentation as a whole group. I like that we work together to find information and then we take turns presenting different points. The fact that I am not the only one out there and I am part of a supportive team makes it fun for me."

Gabriela, 16, BTEC Level 2 First in Performing Arts

"Although presentations are very stressful, when I present my work it helps to hang my ideas together and I find I can express what I want to say more clearly than when I write things down. Instant feedback is helpful and boosts my confidence for the next time."

Ethan, 19, BTEC Level 2 First in Creative Media Production

"I think presentations are useful but I find them difficult to deliver - relying heavily on my memory, which is very nerve-wracking. We were told that presentation would be part of our assessment. I really worried about it and couldn't sleep the night before – stressing out about what I was going to say. I hated the first few minutes, but after that I was OK."

Will, 16, BTEC Level 2 First in Engineering

"I was very nervous about presenting to my class until I took part in the Young Enterprise scheme and had to present the results of our project to over 200 people including the mayor! After that presenting to my class mates didn't feel too nerve wracking at all."

Lizzy, 17, BTEC Level 2 First in Business

"I used to dread presentations on my course, but found that if I went through my notes again and again until I knew the presentation inside out, it made it much easier and the presentations generally went well."

Javinder, 17, BTEC Level 3 National in Construction

Activity: All right on the night?

Read the following account and answer the questions that follow. If possible, compare ideas with a friend in your class.

Gemma looked around in exasperation. The team were on the final rehearsal of their presentation and nothing was going right. Amaya seemed to think it was funny. 'Honestly, Gemma, why don't you just chill for a bit?' she suggested. 'You know what they say – a bad dress rehearsal means we'll do really well tomorrow!'

Gemma glared at her. 'Well, can I make a suggestion, too, Amaya,' she retorted. 'Why don't you just concentrate for a change? Sprawling around and dissolving into giggles every five minutes isn't helping either.'

She turned to Adam. 'And I thought you were going to build a simple model,' she said, 'not one that falls apart every time you touch it.'

Adam looked crest-fallen. 'But I wanted to show how it worked.'

'How it's supposed to work, you mean!' raged Gemma, all her worries and anxieties now coming to the fore. 'We'll look stupid if it ends up in bits on the floor tomorrow and Amaya just falls about laughing again.'

'And Imran,' continued Gemma, turning her sights on the last member of the team, 'why is it so difficult for you to count to three minutes? We've agreed over and over again we'll each talk for three minutes and every time you get carried away with the sound of your own voice and talk for twice as long. It just means we're going to overrun and get penalised. And stop trying to wriggle out of answering questions properly. For heaven's sake, if you don't know the answer, how hard is it just to say so?'

Silence fell. No-one looked at each other. Adam fiddled with his model and something else fell off. Amaya wanted to laugh but didn't dare.

Imran was sulking and vowed never to say anything ever again. 'You wait,' he thought. 'Tomorrow I'll race through my part in one minute flat. And then what will you do?'

1 Identify the strengths and weaknesses of each member of the presentation team.

Name	Strengths	Weaknesses
Gemma		
Amaya		
Adam		
Imran		

2 What have the team done right, so far, in getting ready for their presentation?

3 Why do you think they are having problems?

4 If you were Gemma's tutor, what advice would you give her at this point?

Activity: Preparing your presentation

Like Sally (on page 73), you have been asked to make a presentation on one of the following topics:

- my favourite holiday destination
- my favourite hobby or pastime.

This will be a timed 90-second presentation, and you will be allowed to use visual aids.

Good planning will help to boost your confidence. Choose the topic you want to present and make some planning notes below:

Title
A positive opening to catch everyone's attention. Asking a question can work well eg 'Who likes to …?'
Why your destination or hobby/pastime is so good
A touch of humour?
A strong close …
…..and thank you for listening.

TOP TIPS

When making a PowerPoint presentation, don't just read out what it says on the slides. The audience can do this. Use the slides as prompt cards.

Step Ten: Maximise your opportunities and manage your problems

Case study: Positive or negative?

Zara and Jacob are both studying the BTEC National in Travel and Tourism. Sometimes you wouldn't think they were on the same course. Jacob has a very positive approach to the course, whereas Zara is renowned for being a moaner.

Jacob attends regularly, turns up on time and, although he may not always feel like it, he does keep up with his work most of the time. The work is sometimes hard, but Jacob is not afraid to ask his tutors for help when he needs it. Jacob makes the most of all the trips – he enjoys getting out of the classroom and visiting new places. He also likes it when guest speakers come in to talk to the group about different travel and tourism organisations and jobs. He always asks lots of questions to broaden his knowledge.

Jacob's teamwork is great, and he is in his element getting involved and working with different members of the group. He may not always agree with them but he will always pull his weight. Jacob has volunteered to help out on numerous occasions at open days, and he enjoys telling prospective learners and their parents about the course. He is a great ambassador for the college.

Zara, on the other hand, is not so positive. She sometimes works extra hours in her part-time job and often misses sessions when she feels tired. She then gets behind with her work, misses deadlines, and blames it all on the excessive workload. Sometimes she doesn't understand the work but can be quite defensive, blaming her tutors for not explaining things properly.

Zara often moans on trips and doesn't like many places they visit. She is equally dismissive when a guest speaker talks about job roles or an organisation that she is not interested in. In team tasks Zara can be quite dominant and is not always supportive of others. No wonder some members of the group try to avoid working with her.

Reflection points

Will you adopt Jacob's approach to your course, or are you more like Zara?

If your course takes one or two years to complete, then it is highly likely that you will experience some highs and lows in that time. You may find one or two topics harder than the rest. There may be distractions in your personal life to cope with. All of which means than you may not always be able to do your best.

It is, therefore, sensible to have an action plan to help you cope. It's also wise to plan how to make the best of opportunities for additional experiences or learning. This section shows you how to do this.

TOP TIP

Because life rarely runs smoothly, it's sensible to capitalise on the opportunities that come your way and have a plan to deal with problems.

Making the most of your opportunities

There will be many opportunities for learning on your course, not all of which will be in school or college. You should prepare for some of the following to maximise the opportunities that each offer.

- **External visits**. Prepare in advance by reading about relevant topics. Make notes when you are there. Write up your notes neatly and file them safely for future reference.

- **Visiting speakers**. Questions can usually be submitted to the speaker in advance. Think carefully about information that you would find helpful. Make notes, unless someone has been appointed to make notes for the whole group. You may be asked to thank the speaker on behalf of your group.

- **Work experience**. If work experience is an essential part of your course, your tutor will help you to organise your placement and tell you about the evidence you need to obtain. You may also get a special logbook in which to record your experiences. Read and re-read the units to which your evidence will apply and make sure you understand the grading criteria and what you need to obtain. Make time to write up your notes, logbook and/or diary every night (if possible), while everything is fresh in your mind.

- **In your own workplace**. If you have a full-time or part-time job, watch for opportunities to find out more about relevant topics that relate to your course, such as health and safety, teamwork, dealing with customers, IT security and communications. Your employer will have had to address all of these issues. Finding out more about these issues will broaden your knowledge and give more depth to your assessment responses.

- **Television, newspapers, podcasts and other information sources**. The media can be an invaluable source of information. Look out for news bulletins relating to your studies, as well as information in topical television programmes – from *The Apprentice* to *Top Gear*. You can also read news headlines online (see page 71). Podcasts are useful, too. It will help if you know what topics you will be studying in the months to come, so you can spot useful opportunities as they arise.

TOP TIP

Remember that you can use online catch-up services, such as the BBC iPlayer or 4oD (for Channel 4 shows) to see TV programmes you have missed recently.

Minimising problems

Hopefully, any problems you experience during your course will only be minor; such as struggling to find an acceptable working method with someone in your team.

You should already know who to talk to about these issues, and who to go to if that person is absent or you would prefer to talk to someone else. If your problems are affecting your work, it's sensible to see your tutor promptly. It is a rare learner who is enthusiastic about every topic and gets on well with everyone else doing the course, so your tutor won't be surprised and will give you useful guidance (in confidence) to help.

TOP TIP

Don't delay talking to someone in confidence if you have a serious problem. If your course tutor is unavailable, talk to another staff member instead.

Other sources of help

If you are unfortunate enough to have a more serious personal problem, the following sources of help may be available in your centre.

- **Professional counselling.** There may be a professional counselling service. If you see a counsellor, nothing you say during the session can be mentioned to another member of staff without your permission.

- **Complaint procedures.** If you have a serious complaint, the first step is to talk to your tutor. If you can't resolve your problem informally, there will be a formal learner complaint procedure. These procedures are used only for serious issues, not for minor difficulties.

- **Appeals procedures.** If you disagree with your final grade for an assignment, check the grading criteria and ask the subject tutor to explain how the grade was awarded. If you are still unhappy, talk to your personal tutor. If you still disagree, you have the right to make a formal appeal.

- **Disciplinary procedures.** These exist for when learners consistently flout a centre's rules and ensure that all learners are dealt with in the same way. Hopefully, you will never get into trouble, but you should make sure that you read these procedures carefully to see what could happen if you did. Remember that being honest and making a swift apology is always the wisest course of action.

- **Serious illness.** Whether this involves you, a family member or a close friend, it could affect your attendance. Discuss the problem with your tutor promptly; you will be missing information from the first day you are absent. There are many solutions in this type of situation – such as sending notes by post and updating you electronically (providing you are well enough to cope with the work).

TOP TIP

It's important to know your centre's procedures for dealing with important issues such as complaints, major illnesses, learner appeals and disciplinary matters.

Key points

- Don't miss opportunities to learn more about relevant topics through external visits, listening to visiting speakers, work experience, being at work or even watching television.
- If you have difficulties or concerns, talk to your tutor, or another appropriate person, promptly to make sure your work isn't affected.

Action points

1 Prepare in advance to maximise your opportunities.
   a) List the opportunities available on your course for obtaining more information and talking to experts. You can check with your tutor to make sure you've identified them all.
   b) Check the content of each unit you will be studying so that you know the main topics and focus of each.
   c) Identify the information that may be relevant to your course on television, on radio, in newspapers and in podcasts.

2 Make sure you know how to cope if you have a serious problem.
   a) Check your centre's procedures so you know who to talk to in a crisis, and who to contact if that person is absent.
   b) Find out where you can get hold of a copy of the main procedures in your centre that might affect you if you have a serious problem. Then read them.

Activity: Dealing with problems

There is always someone to turn to when the going gets tough and you have problems to face. Check your student charter and procedures to find out who you would go to if you needed to discuss the following problems or issues:

Issue or problem	Where would you go for help?
You don't think you will achieve the grades you need for university.	
You have no idea what you want to do when you complete your course.	
Your mum has to go into hospital and you will have to take time off college to look after your little brother.	
You believe you should have achieved a higher grade in an assignment.	
One of your tutors always seems to pick on you and shows you up in class when you ask for help.	
You are receiving nasty texts and emails from someone at college.	
You cannot afford the bus fare to come into college every day.	
You are being pressurised by your employer to do more hours at work and it is affecting your college work.	
Another member of the group has borrowed your pen drive and copied your assignments.	
You are working on a group presentation and no-one in your group is pulling their weight.	

AND FINALLY ...

Refer to this Study Skills Guide whenever you need to remind yourself about something related to your course. Keep it in a safe place so that you can use it whenever you need to refresh your memory. That way, you'll get the very best out of your course – and yourself!

TOP TIP

The time and effort you will be putting into this course deserves to be rewarded. Make sure you know how to confront and successfully overcome problems.

Skills building

This section has been written to help you improve the skills needed to do your best in your assignments. You may be excellent at some skills already, others may need further work. The skills you can expect to demonstrate on your course include:

- your personal, learning and thinking skills (**PLTS**)
- your **functional skills** of ICT, maths/numeracy and English
- your proofreading and document production skills.

Personal, learning and thinking skills (PLTS)

These are the skills, personal qualities and behaviour that enable you to operate more independently, work more confidently with other people and be more effective at work. You'll develop these on your BTEC Level 3 National course through a variety of experiences and as you take on different roles and responsibilities.

The skills are divided into six groups.

1 **Independent enquirers** can process and evaluate information they investigate from different perspectives. They can plan what to do and how to do it, and take into account the consequences of making different decisions.

2 **Creative thinkers** generate and explore different ideas. They make connections between ideas, events and experiences that enable them to be inventive and imaginative.

3 **Reflective learners** can assess themselves and other people. They can evaluate their own strengths and limitations. They set themselves realistic goals, monitor their own performance and welcome feedback.

4 **Team workers** collaborate with other people to achieve common goals. They are fair and considerate to others, whether as a team leader or team member, and take account of different opinions.

5 **Self-managers** are well-organised and show personal responsibility, initiative, creativity and enterprise. They look for new challenges and responsibilities and are flexible when priorities change.

6 **Effective participators** play a full part in the life of their school, college, workplace or wider community by taking responsible action to bring improvements for others as well as themselves.

Action points

1 Many parts of this Study Skills Guide relate to the development of your own personal, learning and thinking skills. For each of the following, suggest the main skill groups to which the chapter relates. Refer to the box above and write a number next to each chapter title below.

a) Use your time wisely. ____

b) Understand how to research and analyse information. ____

c) Work productively as a member of a group. ____

d) Understand yourself. ____

e) Utilise all your resources. ____

f) Maximise your opportunities and manage your problems. ____

2 You have been on your BTEC National course for a few months now and, although everyone is enjoying the work, you realise that some of the learners have complaints.

First, several learners object to an increase in the price of printouts and photocopying, on the basis that they can't do good work for their assignments if this is too expensive. You disagree and think that the prices are reasonable, given the cost of paper.

Second, a timetable change means your 2 pm – 4 pm Friday afternoon class has been moved to 9 am – 11 am. Some learners are annoyed and want it changed back, while others are delighted.

a) For the first problem, identify four factors which could indicate that those complaining about the price rise might be justified.

1

2

3

4

b) Now consider the second problem.

  i) Think about which learners in your group would be most affected by the timetable change. Who might be most disturbed? Who might benefit from the earlier start?

  ii) Try to think of a creative solution, or compromise, that would please both groups.

c) During the discussions about these issues, some quieter members of the class are often shouted down by the more excitable members. Suggest a strategy for dealing with this, which everyone is likely to accept.

You can also check your ideas with the suggestions given on page 93.

3 a) Complete the chart opposite, identifying occasions when you may need to demonstrate personal, learning and thinking skills in your future career. Alternatively, apply each area to a part-time job you are currently doing.

b) Identify areas where you think you are quite strong and put a tick in the 'S' column. Check that you could provide evidence to support this judgement, such as a time when you have demonstrated this skill.

c) Now consider areas where you are not so good and put a cross in the 'W' column.

d) Then practise self-management by identifying two appropriate goals to achieve over the next month and make a note of them in the space provided. If possible, talk through your ideas at your next individual tutorial.

Personal, learning and thinking skills for future career/current part-time job				
Skill group	**Example skills**	**Occasions when you use/ will use skill**	**S**	**W**
Independent enquirers	Finding information Solving problems Making decisions Reconciling conflicting information or views Justifying decisions			
Creative thinkers	Finding imaginative solutions Making original connections Finding new ways to do something Opportunities for being innovative and inventive			
Reflective learners	Goals you may set yourself Reviewing your own progress Encouraging feedback Dealing with setbacks or criticism			
Team workers	Working with others Coping with different views to your own Adapting your behaviour Being fair and considerate			
Self-managers	Being self-starting and showing initiative Dealing positively with changing priorities Organising your own time and resources Dealing with pressure Managing your emotions			
Effective participators	Identifying issues of concern to others Proposing ways forward Identifying improvements for others Influencing other people Putting forward a persuasive argument			
Goals	1			
	2			

Functional skills

Functional skills are practical skills that everyone needs to have in order to study and work effectively. They involve using and applying English, maths and ICT.

Improving your literacy skills

Your written English communication skills

A good vocabulary increases your ability to explain yourself clearly. Work that is presented without spelling and punctuation errors looks professional, and increases the likelihood of someone understanding your intended meaning. Your written communication skills will be tested in many assignments. You should work at improving areas of weakness, such as spelling, punctuation or vocabulary.

Try the following ideas to help you improve your written communication skills.

- Read more as this introduces you to new words, and it will help your spelling.

- Look up new words in a dictionary and try to use them in conversation.

- Use a Thesaurus (you can access one electronically in Word) to find alternatives to words you use a lot, this adds variety to your work.

- Never use words you don't understand in the hope that they sound impressive.

- Write neatly, so people can read what you've written.

- Do crosswords to improve your word power and spelling.

- Improve your punctuation – especially the use of apostrophes – either by using an online programme or by using a communication textbook.

- Go to page 94 to find out how to gain access to some helpful websites for this page.

Verbal and non-verbal communication (NVC) skills

Talking appropriately means using the right words and 'tone'; using the right body language means sending positive signals to reinforce this message – such as smiling at someone when you say 'Hello'. Both verbal and non-verbal communication skills are essential when dealing with people at work.

The following ideas are some hints for successful communication.

- Be polite, tactful and sensitive to other people's feelings.

- Think about the words and phrases that you like to hear, and use them when communicating with other people.

- Use simple language so that people can understand you easily. Explain what you mean, when necessary.

- Speak at the right pace. Don't speak so slowly that everyone loses interest, or so fast that no-one can understand you.

- Speak loudly enough for people to hear you clearly – but don't shout!

- Think about the specific needs of different people – whether you are talking to a senior manager, an important client, a shy colleague or an angry customer.

- Recognise the importance of non-verbal communication (NVC) so that you send positive signals by smiling, making eye contact, giving an encouraging nod or leaning forwards to show interest.

- Read other people's body language to spot if they are anxious or impatient so that you can react appropriately.

TOP TIP

Make sure you use the right tone for the person you're talking to. Would you talk to an adult in the same way you'd talk to a very young child?

Action points

1 Go to page 94 to find out how to gain access to websites which can help you to improve your literacy skills.

2 A battery made in China contained the following information.

> **DO NOT CONNECT IMPROPERLY**
>
> **CHARGE OR DISPOSE OF IN FIRE**

a) Can you see any problems with this? Give a reason for your answer.

_____

_____

_____

_____

_____

_____

_____

b) Reword the information so that it is unambiguous.

_____

_____

_____

_____

_____

3 If you ever thought you could completely trust the spellchecker on your computer, type the text given in box A on the next page into your computer. Your spellchecker will not highlight a single error; yet even at a glance you should be able to spot dozens of errors!

Read the passage in box A and try to understand it. Then rewrite it in box B on the next page without spelling, grammatical or punctuation errors. Compare your finished work with the suggested version on page 93.

Box A

Anyone desirable to write books or reports, be they short or long, should strive too maximise they're optimal use of one's English grammar and obliviously there is an need for correct spelling two one should not neglect punctuation neither.

Frequent lea, many people and individuals become confusing or just do not no it, when righting, when words that mean different, when sounding identically, or when pronounced very similar, are knot too bee spelled inn the same whey. The quay two suck seeding is dew care, a lack off witch Leeds too Miss Spellings that mite otherwise of bean a voided. Spell chequers donut find awl missed takes.

Despite all the pitfalls how ever, with practise, patients and the right altitude, any one can soon become a grate writer and speaker, as what I did.

Box B Now rewrite the passage in the space below without errors.

4 In each of the statements listed in the table below suggest what the body language described might mean.

Statement	What might this body language mean?
a) You are talking to your manager when he steps away from you and crosses his arms over his chest.	
b) You are talking to your friend about what she did at the weekend but she's avoiding making eye contact with you.	
c) During a tutorial session, your tutor is constantly tapping his fingers on the arm of his chair.	
d) Whenever you talk to your friend about your next assignment, she bites her lower lip.	

Improving your maths or numeracy skills

If you think numeracy isn't relevant to you, then think again! Numeracy is an essential life skill. If you can't carry out basic calculations accurately then you will have problems, perhaps when you least expect them. You'll often encounter numbers in various contexts – sometimes they will be correctly given, sometimes not. Unless you have a basic understanding about numeracy, you won't be able to tell the difference.

Good numeracy skills will improve your ability to express yourself, especially in assignments and at work. If you have problems, there are strategies that you can practise to help:

- Try to do basic calculations in your head, then check them on a calculator.
- Ask your tutor for help if important calculations give you problems.
- When you are using your computer, use the onscreen calculator (or a spreadsheet package) to do calculations.
- Investigate puzzle sites and brain training software, such as Dr Kageyama's Maths Training by Nintendo.

Action points

1 Go to page 94 to find out how to gain access to websites which can help you to improve your numeracy skills.

2 Try the following task with a friend or family member.

Each of you should write down 36 simple calculations in a list, eg

8 × 6, 19 – 8, 14 + 6.

Exchange lists. See who can answer the most calculations correctly in the shortest time.

3 Figures aren't always what they appear to be. For example, Sophie watches *Who Wants To Be a Millionaire?* She hears Chris Tarrant say

that there have been over 500 shows, with 1200 contestants who have each won over £50,000 on average. Five people have won £1 million.

Sophie says she is going to enter because she is almost certain to win more than £50,000 and could even win a million pounds.

a) On the figures given, what is the approximate total of money won over 500 shows (to the nearest £ million)?

b) Assuming that Sophie is chosen to appear on the show, and makes it on air as a contestant, do you think Sophie's argument that she will 'almost certainly' win more than £50,000 is correct? Give a reason for your answer.

(The correct answer is on page 94.)

4 You have a part-time job and have been asked to carry out a survey on the usage of the drinks vending machine. You decide to survey 500 people, and find that:
- 225 use the machine to buy one cup of coffee per day only
- 100 use the machine to buy one cup of tea per day only
- 75 use the machine to buy one cup of cold drink per day only
- 50 use the machine to buy one cup of hot chocolate per day only
- the rest are non-users
- the ratio of male to female users is 2:1.

a) How many men in your survey use the machine?

b) How many women in your survey use the machine?

c) Calculate the proportion of the people in your survey that use the machine.
Express this as a fraction and as a percentage.

d) What is the ratio of coffee drinkers to tea drinkers in your survey?

e) What is the ratio of coffee drinkers to hot chocolate drinkers in your survey?

f) If people continue to purchase from the machine in the same ratio found in your survey, and last month 1800 cups of coffee were sold, what would you expect the sales of the cold drinks to be?

g) Using the answer to f), if coffee costs 65p and all cold drinks cost 60p, how much would have been spent in total last month on these two items?

Improving your ICT skills

Good ICT skills are an asset in many aspects of your daily life and not just for those studying to be IT practitioners.

These are ways in which you can improve your ICT skills.

- Check that you can use the main features of the software packages you need to produce your assignments, eg Word, Excel and PowerPoint.

- Choose a good search engine and learn to use it properly. For more information, go to page 94 to find out how to access a useful website.

- Developing and using your IT skills enables you to enhance your assignments. This may include learning how to import and export text and artwork from one package to another; taking digital photographs and inserting them into your work and/or creating drawings or diagrams by using appropriate software.

Action points

1 Check your basic knowledge of IT terminology by identifying each of these items on your computer screen:

a) taskbar	**f)** scroll bars
b) toolbar	**g)** status bar
c) title bar	**h)** insertion point
d) menu bar	**i)** maximise/ minimise button.
e) mouse pointer	

2 Assess your IT skills by identifying the packages and operations you find easy to use and those that you find more difficult. If you use Microsoft Office products (Word, PowerPoint, Access or Excel) you can find out more about improving your skills online. Go to page 94 to find out how to access a useful website for this action points section.

3 Search the internet to find a useful dictionary of IT terms. Bookmark it for future use. Find out the meaning of any of the following terms that you don't know already:

a) portal

b) cached link

c) home page

d) browser

e) firewall

f) HTML

g) URL

h) cookie

i) hyperlink

j) freeware.

Proofreading and document preparation skills

Improving your keyboard, document production and general IT skills can save you hours of time. When you have good skills, the work you produce will be of a far more professional standard.

- Think about learning to touch-type. Your centre may have a workshop you can join, or you can use an online program – go to page 94 to find out how to access a web link for this section. From here you can access websites that will allow you to test and work on improving your typing skills.

- Obtain correct examples of any document formats you will have to use, such as a report or summary, either from your tutor, the internet or from a textbook.

- Proofread all your work carefully. A spellchecker won't find all your mistakes, so you must read through it yourself as well.

- Make sure your work looks professional by using a suitable typeface and font size, as well as reasonable margins.

- Print your work and store the printouts neatly, so that it stays in perfect condition for when you hand it in.

Action points

1 You can check and improve your typing skills using online typing sites – see link in previous section.

2 Check your ability to create documents by scoring yourself out of 5 for each of the following questions, where 5 is something you can do easily and 0 is something you can't do at all. Then focus on improving every score where you rated yourself 3 or less.

I know how to:

a) create a new document and open a saved document _____

b) use the mouse to click, double-click and drag objects _____

c) use drop-down menus _____

d) customise my toolbars by adding or deleting options _____

e) save and/or print a document _____

f) create folders and sub-folders to organise my work _____

g) move a folder I use regularly to My Places _____

h) amend text in a document _____

i) select, copy, paste and delete information in a document _____

j) quickly find and replace text in a document _____

k) insert special characters _____

l) create a table or insert a diagram in a document _____

m) change the text size, font and colour _____

n) add bold, italics or underscore _____

o) create a bullet or numbered list _____

p) align text left, right or centred _____

q) format pages before they are printed _____

r) proofread a document so that there are no mistakes _____ .

Answers

Activity: Let's give you a tip... (page 70)

a) i) Fact
ii) Opinion – the number cannot be validated
iii) Fact
iv) Opinion
v) Opinion
vi) Opinion – again the number is estimated

Skills building answers

PLTS action points (page 83)

1 a) Use your time wisely = **5** Self-managers
b) Understand how to research and analyse information = **1** Independent enquirers, **5** Self-managers
c) Work productively as a member of a group = **4** Team workers, **6** Effective participators
d) Understand yourself = **3** Reflective learners
e) Utilise all your resources = **5** Self-managers
f) Maximise your opportunities and manage your problems = **1** Independent enquirers, **2** Creative thinkers, **3** Reflective learners, **5** Self-managers

2 a) Factors to consider in relation to the increased photocopying/printing charges include: the comparative prices charged by other schools/colleges, how often there is a price rise, whether any printing or photocopying at all can be done without charge, whether there are any concessions for special tasks or assignments, the availability of class sets of books/popular library books for loan (which reduces the need for photocopying).

b) i) An earlier start will be more likely to negatively affect those who live further away and who are reliant on public transport, particularly in rural areas. The earlier finish will benefit anyone who has a part-time job that starts on a Friday afternoon or who has after college commitments, such as looking after younger sisters or brothers.

ii) The scope for compromise would depend on whether there are any classes between 11 am and 2 pm on a Friday, whether tutors had any flexibility and whether the new 9 am – 11 am class could be moved to another time or day.

c) One strategy would be to allow discussion for a set time, ensure everyone had spoken, then put the issue to a vote. The leader should prompt suggestions from quieter members by asking people individually what they think.

Literacy skills action points (page 87)

2 a) The statement reads as if it is acceptable to either charge it or dispose of it in fire.
b) Do not connect this battery improperly. Do not recharge it and do not dispose of it in fire.

3 Anyone who wishes to write books or reports, whether short or long, should try to use English grammatically. Obviously there is a need for correct spelling, too. Punctuation should also not be neglected.

Frequently, people confuse words with different meanings when they are writing, especially when these sound identical or very similar, even when they must not be spelled in the same way. The key to succeeding is due care, a lack of which leads to misspellings that might otherwise have been avoided. Spellcheckers do not find all mistakes.

Despite all the pitfalls, however, with practice, patience and the right attitude, anyone can soon become a great writer and speaker, like me.

4 Possible answers.

a) Stepping backwards and crossing arms across the chest might indicate that you manager is creating a barrier between you and himself. This may be because he is angry with you.

b) Your friend may be feeling guilty about what she did at the weekend, or not confident that you will approve of what she tells you.

c) Your tutor might be frustrated as he has many things to do and so wants the tutorial to finish quickly.

d) Your friend might be anxious about the next assignment or about the time she has to complete it.

Numeracy action points (page 90)

3 a) £60 million

b) Sophie's argument is incorrect as £50, 000 is an average, i.e. some contestants will win more, but many will win much less. The distribution of prize money is greater at lower amounts because more people win small amounts of money than large amounts – and only five contestants have won the top prize of £1 million.

4 a) 300

b) 150

c) 9/10ths, 90%

d) 225:100 (= 45:20) = 9:4

e) 225:50 = 9:2

f) 600

g) £1530

Understanding grading criteria (page 20)

Example 1 provides partial evidence for D1 as it provides analysis of the importance of some of the processes at check-in.

Example 2 provides partial evidence for P3 as it outlines of some of the roles and responsibilities of passenger check-in staff.

Example 3 provides partial evidence for M1 as it explains how check-in agents carry out some of their roles and responsibilities.

Accessing website links

Links to various websites are referred to throughout this BTEC Level 3 National Study Skills Guide. To ensure that these links are up-to-date, that they work and that the sites aren't inadvertently linked to any material that could be considered offensive, we have made the links available on our website: www.pearsonhotlinks.co.uk. When you visit the site, please enter the express code 5544S, title BTEC Level 3 National Study Skills Guide in Travel and Tourism or ISBN 9781846905544. From here you can gain access to the website links and information on how they can be used to help you study.

Useful terms

Accreditation of Prior Learning (APL)
Some of your previous achievements and experiences may be able to be used to count towards your qualification.

Apprenticeships
Schemes that enable you to work and earn money at the same time as you gain further qualifications (an NVQ award and a technical certificate) and improve your functional skills. Apprentices learn work-based skills relevant to their job role and their chosen industry. See page 94 for how you can access a website to find out more.

Assessment methods
Techniques used to check that your work demonstrates the learning and understanding required for your qualification, such as assignments, case studies and practical tasks.

Assessor
An assessor is the tutor who marks or assesses your work.

Assignment
A complex task or mini-project set to meet specific grading criteria and learning outcomes.

Awarding body
An organisation responsible for devising, assessing and issuing qualifications. The awarding body for all BTEC qualifications is Edexcel.

Credit value
The number of credits attached to your BTEC course. The credit value increases in relation to the length of time you need to complete the course, from 30 credits for a BTEC Level 3 Certificate, 60 credits for a Subsidiary Diploma, 120 credits for a Diploma, up to 180 credits for an Extended Diploma.

Degrees
Higher education qualifications offered by universities and colleges. Foundation degrees take two years to complete; honours degrees may take three years or longer.

Department for Business Innovation and Skills (BIS)
BIS is responsible for further and higher education and skills training, as well as functions related to trade and industry. See page 94 for how you can access a website to find out more.

Department for Education
The Department for Education is responsible for schools and education, as well as children's services. See page 94 for how you can access a website to find out more.

Distance learning
When you learn and/or study for a qualification at home or at work. You communicate with your tutor and/or the centre that organises the course by post, by telephone or electronically.

Educational Maintenance Award (EMA)
An EMA is a means-tested award that provides eligible learners under 19 who are studying a full-time course at school or college with a cash sum of money every week. See page 94 for how you can access a website to find out more.

External verification
Formal checking of the programme by an Edexcel representative that focuses on sampling various assignments to check content, accurate assessment and grading.

Forbidden combinations
There are some qualifications that cannot be taken simultaneously because their content is too similar.

Functional skills
Practical skills in English, maths and ICT that enable people to work confidently, effectively and independently. Level 2 Functional Skills are mapped to the units of BTEC Level 3 National qualifications. They aren't compulsory to achieve on the course, but are of great use.

Grade boundaries
Pre-set points that determine whether you will achieve a pass, merit or distinction as the overall final grade(s) for your qualification.

Grading criteria
The specific evidence you have to demonstrate to obtain a particular grade in the unit.

Grading domains
The main areas of learning that support the learning outcomes. On a BTEC Level 3 National course these are: application of knowledge and understanding; development of practical and technical skills; personal development for occupational roles; application of PLTS and functional skills.

Grading grid
The table in each unit of your qualification specification that sets out what you have to show you can do.

Higher education (HE)
Post-secondary and post-further education, usually provided by universities and colleges.

Higher-level skills
These are skills such as evaluating or critically assessing information. They are more difficult than lower-level skills such as writing a description or making a list. You must be able to demonstrate higher-level skills to achieve a distinction.

Indicative reading
Recommended books and journals whose content is both suitable and relevant for the BTEC unit studied.

Induction
A short programme of events at the start of a course designed to give you essential information and introduce you to your fellow learners and tutors, so that you can settle down as quickly and easily as possible.

Internal verification
The quality checks carried out by nominated tutors at your school or college to ensure that all assignments are at the right level and cover appropriate learning outcomes and grading criteria, and that all assessors are marking work consistently and to the same standard.

Investors in People (IiP)
A national quality standard that sets a level of good practice for training and developing of people within a business. Participating organisations must demonstrate commitment to achieving the standard.

Learning outcomes
The knowledge and skills you must demonstrate to show that you have effectively learned a unit.

Learning support
Additional help that is available to all learners in a school or college who have learning difficulties or other special needs.

Levels of study
The depth, breadth and complexity of knowledge, understanding and skills required to achieve a qualification, which also determine its level. Level 2 equates to GCSE level and Level 3 equates to A-level. As you successfully achieve one level, you can then progress to the next. BTEC qualifications are offered at Entry Level, then Levels 1, 2, 3, 4 and 5.

Local Education Authority (LEA)
The local government body responsible for providing education for all learners of compulsory school age. The LEA is also responsible for managing the education budget for 16–19-year-old learners in its area.

Mandatory units
These are units that all learners must complete to gain a qualification, in this case a BTEC Level 3 National. Some BTEC qualifications have an over-arching title, eg Construction, but within Construction you can choose different pathways. Your chosen pathway may have additional mandatory units specific to that pathway.

Mentor
A more experienced person who will guide you and counsel you if you have a problem or difficulty.

Mode of delivery
The way in which a qualification is offered to learners, for example part-time, full-time, as a short course or by distance learning.

National Occupational Standard (NOS)
Statements of the skills, knowledge and understanding you need to develop in order to be competent at a particular job.

National Vocational Qualification (NVQ)
Qualifications that concentrate on the practical skills and knowledge required to do a job competently. They are usually assessed in the workplace and range from Level 1 (the lowest) to Level 5 (the highest).

Nested qualifications
Qualifications that have 'common' units, so that learners can easily progress from one to another by adding on more units

Ofqual
The public body responsible for regulating qualifications, exams and tests in England.

Optional units
Units on your course from which you may be able to make a choice. They help you specialise your skills, knowledge and understanding, and may help progression into work or further education.

Pathway
All BTEC Level 3 National qualifications comprise a small number of mandatory units and a larger number of optional units. These units are grouped into different combinations to provide alternative pathways to achieving the qualification. These pathways are usually linked to different career preferences.

Peer review
This involves feedback on your performance by your peers (members of your team or class group.) You will also be given an opportunity to review their performance.

Plagiarism
The practice of copying someone else's work or work from any other sources (eg the internet), and passing it off as your own. This practice is strictly forbidden on all courses.

Personal, learning and thinking skills (PLTS)
The skills, personal qualities and behaviour that improve your ability to work independently. Developing these skills makes you more effective and confident at work. Opportunities for developing these skills are a feature of all BTEC Level 3 National courses. These skills aren't compulsory to achieve on the course, but are of great use to you.

Portfolio
A collection of work compiled by a learner, usually as evidence of learning, to present to an assessor.

Procrastinator
Someone who is forever putting off or delaying work, either because they are lazy or because they have poor organisational skills.

Professional body
An organisation that exists to promote or support a particular profession, for example the Royal Institute of British Architects (RIBA).

Professional development and training
This involves undertaking activities relevant to your job to increase and/or update your knowledge and skills.

Project
A project is a comprehensive piece of work, which normally involves original research and investigation by an individual or by a team. The findings and results may be presented in writing and summarised as a presentation.

Qualifications and Credit Framework (QCF)
The QCF is a framework for recognising skills and qualifications. It does this by awarding credit for qualifications and units so that they are easier to measure and compare. All BTEC Level 3 National qualifications are part of the QCF.

Qualifications and Curriculum Development Agency (QCDA)
The QCDA is responsible for maintaining and developing the national curriculum, delivering assessments, tests and examinations, and reforming qualifications.

Quality assurance
In education, this is the process of continually checking that a course of study is meeting the specific requirements set down by the awarding body.

Sector Skills Councils (SSCs)
The 25 employer-led, independent organisations responsible for improving workforce skills in the UK by identifying skill gaps and improving learning in the workplace. Each council covers a different type of industry.

Semester
Many universities and colleges divide their academic year into two halves or semesters, one from September to January and one from February to July.

Seminar
A learning event involving a group of learners and a tutor, which may be learner-led, and may follow research into a topic that has been introduced at an earlier stage.

Study buddy

A person in your group or class who takes notes for you and keeps you informed of important developments if you are absent. You do the same for them in return.

Time-constrained assignment

An assessment you must complete within a fixed time limit.

Tutorial

An individual or small group meeting with your tutor at which you can discuss your current work and other more general course issues. At an individual tutorial, your progress on the course will be discussed and you can raise any concerns or personal worries you may have.

The University and Colleges Admissions Service (UCAS)

UCAS (pronounced 'you-cass') is the central organisation that processes all applications for higher education (HE) courses.

UCAS points

The number of points allocated by UCAS for the qualifications you have obtained. Higher education institutions specify how many points you need to be accepted on the courses they offer. See page 94 for how you can access a website to find out more.

Unit abstract

The summary at the start of each BTEC unit that tells you what the unit is about.

Unit content

Details about the topics covered by the unit and the knowledge and skills you need to complete it.

Unit points

The number of points you gain when you complete a unit. These will depend on the grade you achieve (pass, merit or distinction).

Vocational qualification

Designed to develop knowledge and understanding relevant to a chosen area of work.

Work experience

Time you spend on an employer's premises when you learn about the enterprise, carry out work-based tasks, and develop skills and knowledge.

Please note that all information given within these useful terms was correct at the time of going to print.